✔ KU-033-346

COLLINS
SECOND
QUIZ
BOOK

Alistair Fyfe

HarperCollinsPublishers

HarperCollinsPublishers
P. O. Box, Glasgow G4 0NB
www.**fire**and**water**.com

© HarperCollinsPublishers 1998

Reprint 10 9 8 7 6 5 4 3 2 1

ISBN 0 00 472 200 0

A catalogue record for this book is available from the British Library

All rights reserved

Printed in Great Britain by
Caledonian International Book Manufacturing Ltd, Glasgow G64

CONTENTS

HOW TO USE THIS BOOK

This is the second edition of the successful Collins *Quiz Book*. Like its predecessor, it is simply designed and easy to use.

QUESTIONS
Each of 120 pages has a set of questions covering aspects of popular knowledge and culture. Ten of the questions fall into specific categories, while the eleventh in each set, the 'True or False?' question, can be used either as a tie-breaker or just as a regular question.

ANSWERS
The answers page-number for each set is flagged at the foot of its questions page. In some answers, especially in the 'True or False?' category, part of the answer appears in brackets. This is simply given as extra information and is not essential to answer the question correctly – although you can use it that way, if you want to give your quiz a harder edge.

Have fun with the questions, and good luck!

SECTION ONE

THE QUIZ BOOK QUESTIONS

SETS 1 – 120

Food & Drink
The name of which liqueur literally translates as 'the drink that satisfies'?

Natural World
What country uses a dram as a unit of currency?

History
How many prime ministers, including Tony Blair, have there been in the present queen's reign?

Culture & Belief
What would be your special subject if you studied apiology?

Stage & Screen
Which Tellytubby carries a red handbag?

Written Word
What was the name of the bowler-hatted, sober-suited brothers in *Tin Tin*?

Music
At first sight, what was unusual about the 1980s pop group The Thompson Twins?

Famous People
During the BSE scare, what government minister made his daughter eat burgers for a photo-call?

Sport & Leisure
What modern-day pub game was originally introduced into America by the Pilgrim Fathers?

Science & Tech
Which children's toy was invented in 1900 by Frank Hornby?

True or False?
Germany's Oktoberfest beer festival always begins in September; true or false?

ANSWERS: PAGE 131

Food & Drink
What country holds the record for largest consumption of alcoholic spirits?

 Natural World
What made Milwaukee famous?

 History
What does the Woolsack symbolise?

 Culture & Belief
Who sits on the Woolsack in the House of Lords?

 Stage & Screen
What is the name of the green Tellytubby?

 Written Word
Whose dog was Snowy?

 Music
What two colours featured in a 1955 hit for Eddie Calvert?

 Famous People
Mel Blanc, the voice of Bugs Bunny, was allergic to what?

 Sport & Leisure
On a Monopoly board, what colour is Old Kent Road?

 Science & Tech
In a British electric plug, what colour is the live wire?

 True or False?
Eating carrots helps you see in the dark; true or false?

ANSWERS: PAGE 131

Food & Drink How much sugar does the average Briton eat every month?

Natural World Canterbury Cathedral is in which county?

History What modern European capital was established by the Moors in the 10th century as Medina Majerit?

Culture & Belief Which city's art gallery is the Prado?

Stage & Screen What comedy-drama programme features a dog called Diefenbacker?

Written Word According to T. S. Eliot, what is April?

Music What was the nickname of R&B musician Antoine Domino?

Famous People Where was Archbishop Thomas Beckett murdered in the 12th century?

Sport & Leisure How many pieces in a domino set have a six on them?

Science & Tech Which pin on a three pin plug is the longest?

True or False? Writer Arthur Conan Doyle created the first fictional detective; true or false?

ANSWERS: PAGE 132

Food & Drink
How many lumps of sugar are in a can of non-diet fizzy drink?

Natural World
Which sex of elephants have tusks – male or female?

History
What addition was once made to army uniforms to stop soldiers wiping their noses on their sleeves?

Culture & Belief
Which church's great bell is the largest in the UK?

Stage & Screen
How much were actress Betty Grable's renowned 'million dollar legs' actually insured for?

Written Word
Which Victorian detective described his toughest cases as 'three-pipe problems'?

Music
Which of the three Bee Gees is the youngest?

Famous People
Louis Farrakhan is a leader of which organisation?

Sport & Leisure
Which animal appears on the badges of both Dumbarton FC and Coventry FC?

Science & Tech
What are the three primary colours for artists?

True or False?
Legendary sleuth Sherlock Holmes played the saxophone; true or false?

ANSWERS: PAGE 132

Food & Drink
What else would you call bovine spongiform encephalopothy?

Natural World
What is known as the lungs of New York City?

History
What job did Joseph Goebbels do in Adolph Hitler's Nazi government?

Culture & Belief
What hand does the Statue of Liberty hold her torch in?

Stage & Screen
Name the five members of the Simpsons family.

Written Word
Why did Mae West advise you should keep a diary?

Music
What 1970 tune, now reinstated, was the original theme music for *Top Of The Pops*?

Famous People
The two most infamous sex scandals of the Victorian Era both involved Irishmen; name one of them.

Sport & Leisure
What is the height of a badminton net?

Science & Tech
How many colours are generated by a colour TV tube?

True or False?
The three primary colours are red, green and blue; true or false?

ANSWERS: PAGE 133

Food & Drink — What is tofu made of?

 Natural World — One of the two ancient granite obelisks called Cleopatra's Needles is in London; where is the other?

 History — Who did the original Peeping Tom peep at in 1040?

 Culture & Belief — The Statue of Liberty holds a torch in one hand; what is in the other?

 Stage & Screen — Who is the sidekick of Mr Burns, head of Springfield's nuclear plant, in *The Simpsons*?

 Written Word — What boffin's equation A=X+Y+Z gave A as success, X as work, Y play, and Z keeping your mouth shut?

 Music — Who first had a hit with *Whole Lotta Love*?

 Famous People — Lady Godiva rode naked through Coventry in which century?

 Sport & Leisure — In what field competition are the winners those who move backwards most effectively?

 Science & Tech — What is the Statue of Liberty made of?

True or False? — Adolf Hitler took his pet rat, Otto, with him everywhere he went; true or false?

ANSWERS: PAGE 133

Food & Drink　Which vegetable is the basis of quorn?

Natural World　How much skin, to the nearest two square feet, does an average-sized man have?

History　How many of his wives did Henry VIII divorce?

Culture & Belief　Which three of the seven virtues are regarded as being the most important?

Stage & Screen　What brunette starred alongside Marilyn Monroe in the film *Gentlemen Prefer Blondes*?

Written Word　According to Anita Loos, who do gentlemen marry?

Music　'Paul' is Paul McCartney's second name; what is his first?

Famous People　How old was Marilyn Monroe when she died?

Sport & Leisure　How many gold medals did the UK win in the 1996 Olympic Games?

Science & Tech　What was the name of the world's first clone of an adult animal?

True or False?　The Beatles were the first British group to have a number 1 hit in the USA; true or false?

ANSWERS: PAGE 134

Food & Drink
What did Shirley Conran say life is too short to do?

Natural World
How many pairs of ribs do humans have?

History
Three of Henry VIII's six wives shared a name; what was it?

Culture & Belief
In the Book of Genesis, where did the Land of Nod lie?

Stage & Screen
Name two of the three women who originally appeared in the '70s TV series, *Charlie's Angels*.

Written Word
What sibling asked 'Am I my brother's keeper?'

Music
What famous Beatles song was supposedly based on a fantastical painting by John Lennon's son Julian?

Famous People
What famous musician owns a film company called Handmade Films?

Sport & Leisure
Where were the 1944 Olympic Games supposed to be held?

Science & Tech
What mathematical sign is used to describe the ratio of a circle's circumference to its diameter?

True or False?
Vera Lynn was the first British female singer to have a number 1 hit in the USA; true or false?

ANSWERS: PAGE 134

Food & Drink

What is the source of the red food colouring cochineal?

Natural World

What insect's bite can spread malaria?

History

How many of Henry VIII's wives outlived him?

Culture & Belief

How many months are there in the Hindu calendar?

Stage & Screen

What were Ned, Min and Bluebottle better known as?

Written Word

What demonic name means 'Lord of the Flies'?

Music

What group cancelled their 1998 UK tour because of their projected tax bill?

Famous People

Who sailed yachts called *Gipsy Moth*?

Sport & Leisure

What was so unusual about Abebe Bikila's winning run in the 1960 Olympic Marathon?

Science & Tech

What number is pi (π) usually given?

True or False?

In 1995-6, the Beatles earned more money than the Rolling Stones; true or false?

ANSWERS: PAGE 135

Food & Drink
A cake baked at 350°F would need what number on a gas cooker?

Natural World
Which chromosome from its father determines whether a baby will be a girl, X or Y?

History
How was Henry VIII of England related to James IV of Scotland?

Culture & Belief
Who was the Norse god of Thunder?

Stage & Screen
In the *Star Wars* movies, what was Darth Vader's name before he went to the Dark Side of the Force?

Written Word
What film was based on the story *Do Androids Dream of Electric Sheep*?

Music
Who recorded a record-breaking album called *Songs for Swingin' Lovers*?

Famous People
What rival once said of Frank Sinatra 'He had the voice of a lifetime. Unfortunately, it's my lifetime'?

Sport & Leisure
Who was accused of tripping US runner Mary Decker-Slaney in the 1984 Olympic 5000m race?

Science & Tech
Who invented the centigrade thermometer?

True or False?
The Volkswagen Beetle was designed by a Herr Porsche; true or false?

ANSWERS: PAGE 135

Food & Drink
What substance in tea is a passion killer?

Natural World
How many pairs of chromosomes does a human cell contain?

History
In Shakespeare's play, Hamlet stabs Polonius through the arras; what is an arras?

Culture & Belief
What do the initials T&GWU stand for?

Stage & Screen
What county is the long-running BBC radio series *The Archers* set in?

Written Word
What is the most filmed Shakespeare play?

Music
What is the connection between the bands Bananarama and Shakespear's Sister?

Famous People
Who won an Oscar for his role as Private Angelo Maggio in the 1953 film *From Here to Eternity*?

Sport & Leisure
What country won football's first World Cup in 1930?

Science & Tech
Where was the ill-fated cruise ship *Titanic* built?

True or False?
Hamlet has the most lines of all Shakespeare's characters; true or false?

ANSWERS: PAGE 136

Food & Drink What is the English term for the dish the Italians call *Zuppa Inglese*?

Natural World In what modern-day country is the ancient city of Carthage?

History What is the only instance of the George Cross ever having been awarded to an entire population?

Culture & Belief What is the second-highest British gallantry award?

Stage & Screen What is the name of the character revealed to be *The Third Man*?

Written Word What kind of animal was Beatrix Potter's Mrs Tiggywinkle?

Music In the song, what do The Crystal Chandeliers light up?

Famous People What youthful film prodigy claimed that he had started at the top and worked down?

Sport & Leisure What race commemorates the arrival in ancient Athens of news of a victory over the Persians?

Science & Tech Where in Britain is there a miniature copy of the Eiffel Tower?

True or False? The Eiffel Tower was designed by a Mr Eiffel; true or false?

ANSWERS: PAGE 136

Food & Drink
What type of dish is bouillabaisse?

Natural World
What part of the eye determines its colour?

History
How many pre-decimal pennies was a florin worth?

Culture & Belief
What, according to the proverb, do listeners never hear?

Stage & Screen
What film features a central scene at the top of the big wheel in a deserted Viennese funfair?

Written Word
In the story *The Three Billy Goats Gruff*, what fearsome creature was hiding under the bridge?

Music
In the song *Jailhouse Rock*, what did the warder tell Sad Sack to use instead of a partner?

Famous People
What publishing tycoon's life was reputedly the inspiration for the film *Citizen Kane*?

Sport & Leisure
How many Formula 1 races had Mika Hakkinen won before the 1998 Grand Prix race season?

Science & Tech
How tall, to the nearest 10 ft, is London's St Paul's Cathedral?

True or False?
Jackie Stewart won more grand prix races than Nigel Mansell; true or false?

ANSWERS: PAGE 137

Food & Drink

What kind of sauce is the basis for tartare sauce?

Natural World

A liger is a cross between which two animals?

History

How many decimal pennies was a florin worth at the time of decimalisation?

Culture & Belief

When poverty comes in at the door, what does the proverb say flies out of the window?

Stage & Screen

Who was Diana Rigg's predecessor as John Steed's sidekick in *The Avengers*?

Written Word

What is the name of the little boy in the *Winnie-the-Pooh* stories?

Music

What band was Louise a member of before leaving to go solo?

Famous People

Who said 'in the future everyone will be world famous for 15 minutes'?

Sport & Leisure

Who were the second Scottish football team to win nine successive league championships?

Science & Tech

Which is the only one of the seven wonders of the Ancient World still in existence?

True or False?

The MGM lion is named Leo; true or false?

ANSWERS: PAGE 137

Food & Drink
What drink should be colourless, odourless and tasteless?

Natural World
What is the least amount of rain likely to fall on Brazil's rainforest in a year (to the nearest 10 in)?

History
How many military Crusades were fought to take the Holy Land between 1096 and 1204?

Culture & Belief
In the zodiac, what are the three water signs?

Stage & Screen
Who runs the Post Office in Postman Pat's village, Greendale?

Written Word
What aquatic-sounding Chinese novel and TV series tells of Robin Hood-type bandits fighting corruption?

Music
What did my true love send to me on the seventh day of Christmas?

Famous People
The Lake District town of Grasmere was home to what well-loved poet?

Sport & Leisure
Which swimming event was introduced to the Olympics in LA in 1984?

Science & Tech
What is an Archimedes screw used to lift?

True or False?
French Perrier Water was originally produced by an Englishman; true or false?

ANSWERS: PAGE 138

Food & Drink

What type of pastry is used to make Mille Feuille?

Natural World

What US city's nickname is the 'Windy City'?

History

What foreign-born monarch began the building of the Tower of London?

Culture & Belief

What do seven magpies signify, according to the old rhyme?

Stage & Screen

What actor writes and plays TV's Alan Partridge?

Written Word

What poet's love was like a red, red rose?

Music

What song has the lines 'He rattled his marracas close to me, In no time I was trembling at the knees'?

Famous People

How many times was Charles de Gaulle president of France – two, three or four?

Sport & Leisure

Where are the Commonwealth Games due to be held in 2002?

Science & Tech

What building in London is set at exactly 0 degrees longitude?

True or False?

On the London Underground every year, more single gloves are lost than pairs of gloves; true or false?

ANSWERS: PAGE 138

Food & Drink What does Mille Feuille mean?

 Natural World To the nearest thousand miles, how far is Peking from Buenos Aires?

 History When was the first city sewer devised – 600 BC, 200 BC or 100 AD?

 Culture & Belief According to Arthurian legend, who, as well as Arthur, loved Guinevere?

 Stage & Screen Who produced the classic Western *The Wild Bunch*?

 Written Word What did Neil Kinnock say was the most important book in the Tory education system?

 Music Three of the members of Abba were called Agnetha, Bjorn and Benny; who was the fourth?

 Famous People What was the previous job of TV presenter Robert Kilroy-Silk?

 Sport & Leisure What game would you be playing if you played spoilfive?

 Science & Tech What river does the world's longest bridge span?

 True or False? The pigtail was banned in China in the early 20th century; true or false?

ANSWERS: PAGE 139

Food & Drink

What robust cheese might you be served alongside port?

Natural World

What is the famous English village set entirely in a prehistoric stone circle?

History

What was the name of Butch Cassidy and the Sundance Kid's gang?

Culture & Belief

What is the largest sculpture in Britain?

Stage & Screen

What classic film was the '70s TV series *Alias Smith and Jones* based on?

Written Word

Why did Jane Eyre not marry Mr Rochester at the first attempt?

Music

What stirring anthem originally went under the less-than-snappy title *War Song for the Rhine Army*?

Famous People

What opera singer was romantically involved for years with Artistotle Onassis?

Sport & Leisure

Who won the Tour de France in 1998?

Science & Tech

Bibendum is the French name for which trademark creature?

True or False?

The word guillotine came from an amalgamation of the French words for 'neck' and 'sever'; true or false?

ANSWERS: PAGE 139

Food & Drink What turns the blue veins in cheese blue?

 Natural World What two countries share the West Indian island of Hispaniola?

 History What country did dictators Papa Doc and Baby Duvalier rule for almost 30 years?

 Culture & Belief What traditionally is thanks given for at Thanksgiving Day in the US?

 Stage & Screen Name one of the two adult dalmatians in *101 Dalmatians*.

 Written Word If a play is described as Shavian, what does this tell you about it?

 Music What is Irish singer-songwriter George Ivan better known as?

 Famous People What 20th-century wit was said to have declared 'Television is for appearing on, not looking at'?

 Sport & Leisure What four tournaments comprise golf's Grand Slam?

 Science & Tech Diesel for farm machinery is taxed differently from DERV. How can you tell them apart?

 True or False? The Channel Tunnel is the world's longest underwater tunnel; true or false?

ANSWERS: PAGE 140

Food & Drink
If you ordered pastrami on rye, what would you be served?

Natural World
Where is the ocean of storms?

History
What country's flag reached the moon first?

Culture & Belief
What star sign was Jesus Christ?

Stage & Screen
What is the name of Mickey Mouse's dog?

Written Word
In *1984* by George Orwell, who is the dictator of Oceania?

Music
Which Dean Martin hit starts 'When the moon hits your eye like a big pizza pie'?

Famous People
Name one of the two late 'spaced-out' celebrities who took part in the first-ever space burial in 1997.

Sport & Leisure
How many times has Seve Ballesteros won the British Open golf tournament?

Science & Tech
How many planets are in our solar system?

True or False?
Joan Collins once appeared as the captain's love interest in *Star Trek – The Next Generation*; true or false?

ANSWERS: PAGE 140

Food & Drink — What colour are pistachio nuts?

Natural World — What group of islands does Fair Isle belong to?

History — What well-loved British institution clocked up its half-century in 1998?

Culture & Belief — What event are hot cross buns supposed to commemorate?

Stage & Screen — Who played the part of Fagin in the 1968 film *Oliver!*?

Written Word — What legendary film reviewer said *'Frankenstein* and *My Fair Lady* are really the same story'?

Music — Who is Paul McCartney's musician brother?

Famous People — Who was the Queen's unexpected companion in her bedchamber in July 1982?

Sport & Leisure — Ice hockey is the national sport of what country?

Science & Tech — Which textile is only genuine if handwoven in the Outer Hebrides?

True or False? — The Shetland pony is the smallest breed of horse; true or false?

ANSWERS: PAGE 141

Food & Drink
Which ingredient in some toothpastes is also used to make scones rise?

 Natural World
How many teeth does an adult human have?

 History
What was special about the sailing of the ship *Empire Windrush* to Britain in 1948?

 Culture & Belief
What festival is celebrated three days after Maundy Thursday?

 Stage & Screen
What type of product was featured on the first TV commercial?

 Written Word
What pirate had a parrot that cried 'Pieces of eight! Pieces of eight!'?

 Music
What wacky '60s band featured both Mike McGear and poet Roger McGough?

 Famous People
Which Pacific island eventually became home to Scottish author Robert Louis Stevenson?

 Sport & Leisure
When was the Wimbledon Tennis Championship opened to professionals?

 Science & Tech
How many degrees has each angle in an equilateral triangle?

True or False?
If your diet consisted only of rabbit meat, you would die of vitamin deficiency; true or false?

ANSWERS: PAGE 141

Food & Drink

The MAFF regulates food labelling. What does MAFF stand for?

Natural World

What is the only country in the world where half of all citizens are classified as being overweight?

History

What date is inscribed on the book held by the Statue of Liberty?

Culture & Belief

If an American told you he had just swallowed a goofball, what would you expect him to do?

Stage & Screen

What lollipop-sucking cop from the 1970s had the catchphrase 'Who loves ya, baby'?

Written Word

In Shakespeare's play, why did Julius Caesar dislike Cassius' appearance?

Music

Name two of the three members of the enduringly influential 1960s band Cream.

Famous People

What name was super-slim model and actress Lesley Hornby better known by?

Sport & Leisure

What is the maximum weight of a flyweight boxer?

Science & Tech

How many sides has a trapezium?

True or False?

The USA consumes more sweets annually per head of population than Denmark; true or false?

ANSWERS: PAGE 142

12116000
322 / 933

Gunpowder can be what kind of drink?

 What American state is Montpelier the capital of?

 What is the significance of the date 1776 inscribed on the Statue of Liberty's book?

 What nationality was the Good Samaritan of the Bible story?

 What two TV series do the characters Bob Ferris and Terry Collier appear in?

 What was the name of Long John Silver's parrot?

 What was the record chosen in 1973 to launch Richard Branson's new Virgin label?

 What did the navigator Amerigo Vespucci give his name to?

 How often is yachting's America's Cup held?

 What country had the better-quality high-definition TV first – USA or UK?

 All the tea in China is less than all the tea in India; true or false?

ANSWERS: PAGE 142

Food & Drink What type of fruit is ananas another name for?

 Natural World What is the non-technical name for the sternum?

 History What early American president is pictured on the one-dollar bill?

 Culture & Belief Which of Hercules' tasks ultimately caused his death?

 Stage & Screen What famous British cartoonist drew the characters in Disney's animated feature film *Hercules?*

 Written Word What was the name of Noddy's house?

 Music What two brothers formed the backbone of the 1960s group The Kinks?

 Famous People What famous artist is married to actress and cake-maker Jane Asher?

 Sport & Leisure Who recorded snooker's first official maximum break, in 1955?

 Science & Tech How is the clavicle commonly known?

 True or False? Per head of population, the UK drinks more tea than Ireland; true or false?

ANSWERS: PAGE 143

Food & Drink
What do vichyssoise and gazpacho have in common?

Natural World
What is the name of the sleep stage when dreaming occurs?

History
What London street was synonymous with fashion in the 1960s?

Culture & Belief
How many years would you be married if you were celebrating your lace anniversary?

Stage & Screen
What Hollywood star first found fame on the classic TV western series *Rawhide*?

Written Word
Who wrote the original book *A Clockwork Orange*?

Music
What did Molly Malone cry in the streets of Dublin?

Famous People
Which acclaimed English actor began his TV career on the 1970s children's programme *Playaway*?

Sport & Leisure
What team has won the World Cup more than any other?

Science & Tech
What distinction did Valentina Tereshkova achieve in 1963?

True or False?
One person in every five on Earth is Chinese; true or false?

ANSWERS: PAGE 143

Food & Drink
Which between vodka and red wine will give a worse hangover?

Natural World
What do the initials REM stand for?

History
What was unusual about 19th-century British prime minister Spencer Percival?

Culture & Belief
What would an Irishman do in a boreen?

Stage & Screen
What TV character's catchphrase was 'Drink! Feck! Arse! Girls!'?

Written Word
What foot did Dubliner Christy Brown kick with in the book and double-Oscar-winning 1989 film?

Music
Who took the hit song *Things Can Only Get Better* as their theme song in 1997?

Famous People
Which one of his senior Labour Party colleagues did Denis Healey liken to a garden gnome?

Sport & Leisure
How many countries have won the World Cup?

Science & Tech
How many units of alcohol are there in a 70cl bottle of 40% proof whisky?

True or False?
Neil Armstrong first stepped onto the moon with his right foot; true or false?

ANSWERS: PAGE 144

Food & Drink — Which spirit is made by distilling wine?

 Natural World — What distinguishes marsupials from other mammals?

 History — What town was obliterated by an eruption of Vesuvius in 79 AD?

 Culture & Belief — What would be the interest someone interested in hostelaphily?

 Stage & Screen — What TV programme does Assistant Director Walter Skinner appear in?

 Written Word — What is the name of the garage-owner in the Noddy stories?

 Music — Who was George Michael's partner in Wham!?

 Famous People — Film directors Fellini, Bogdanovich, Godard and Huston all shared the same original job; what was it?

 Sport & Leisure — What team was the only one to remain unbeaten in the 1974 World Cup?

 Science & Tech — How many units of alcohol is considered a safe weekly limit for women?

True or False? — 'X' is the least-used letter in the English Alphabet; true or false?

ANSWERS: PAGE 144

Food & Drink
What name is commonly given to the indigestible substance also known as cellulose or fibre?

Natural World
What type of bird do sailors call a gooney bird?

History
What has been banned from British television since 1 August 1965?

Culture & Belief
Do British male subjects have to bow to the Queen?

Stage & Screen
What two of TV's *Friends* characters are brother and sister in the programme?

Written Word
What does Noddy do for a living?

Music
How was Peter & Gordon's 1964 US no. 1 *World Without Love* important for Lennon & McCartney?

Famous People
Which pop group still features in the top ten highest earning entertainers, 25 years after splitting up?

Sport & Leisure
What is a poop deck?

Science & Tech
Which organ of the body is affected by cirrhosis?

True or False?
Cigarettes are the most popular duty-free purchase; true or false?

ANSWERS: PAGE 145

Food & Drink
What percentage of the fibre we eat is absorbed by the body?

Natural World
What colour is the gemstone citrine?

History
What made the Sinn Fein MP Constance Markievicz notable in British political history?

Culture & Belief
What would you be afraid of if you suffered from venustaphobia?

Stage & Screen
What kind of girls were Pussy Galore, Mary Goodnight and Kissy Suzuki?

Written Word
In what Ian Fleming novel was Bond's preference for martini 'shaken not stirred' first noted?

Music
Who came from a land down under to have a simultaneous hit in the UK and US in 1982?

Famous People
What quizmaster first played James Bond, in a radio production?

Sport & Leisure
What type of sailing boat is the fastest?

Science & Tech
Au is the symbol of which element?

True or False?
In the Gulf state Qatar, men outnumber women by almost two to one; true or false?

ANSWERS: PAGE 145

Food & Drink
Potatoes contain a significant amount of which vitamin?

Natural World
How many million years old is the earth thought to be, to the nearest 500?

History
What period in American history does antebellum refer to?

Culture & Belief
Name any one of the three creeds declaring the Christian faith.

Stage & Screen
What children's radio series began with the words 'Are you sitting comfortably? Then I'll begin'?

Written Word
According to the King James Bible, who was Lucifer?

Music
Which Radio 2 DJ had two number 1 hits in the 1950s?

Famous People
George Washington was the first American president; who was the second?

Sport & Leisure
Where would you expect to see athletes Hunter, Wolf and Lightning?

Science & Tech
How much does a litre of water weigh?

True or False?
John F Kennedy was the first Catholic president of the US; true or false?

ANSWERS: PAGE 146

Food & Drink
Vitamin D is only found in foods which contain what?

Natural World
What city does the Isis flow through?

History
What was National Socialist German Workers' Party better known as in the 1930s?

Culture & Belief
The Greek goddess of hunting was called Artemis; what name did the Romans give her?

Stage & Screen
Which Disney character was named after a newly discovered planet in 1930?

Written Word
In what year was the *Highway Code* first published: 1927, 1929 or 1931?

Music
What pop group appeared in the film *The Great Rock & Roll Swindle*?

Famous People
Who said 'I love Mickey Mouse more than any woman I've ever known'?

Sport & Leisure
Name one of the two Thames bridges that the University Boat Race passes under.

Science & Tech
The world's first traffic lights were in London; when did they date from (within five years)?

True or False?
There is a city called Rome on every continent; true or false?

ANSWERS: PAGE 146

Food & Drink
What is marmite?

Natural World
What collective noun describes both a group of kangaroos and a group of monkeys?

History
What is the oldest British order of chivalry?

Culture & Belief
What would an Australian do with a billabong – play it, eat it or paddle in it?

Stage & Screen
What is unusual about the films directed by 'Alan Smithee'?

Written Word
What American writer coined the phrase 'the beat generation'?

Music
What did the Jolly Swagman from *Waltzing Matilda* camp in the shade of?

Famous People
Which famous film director appeared in a bit part in *The Blues Brothers*?

Sport & Leisure
What was tennis player Evonne Cawley's maiden name?

Science & Tech
What European city was home to the world's first contraceptive clinic in 1881?

True or False?
Spiral staircases in medieval buildings were always built clockwise; true or false?

ANSWERS: PAGE 147

Food & Drink
What American town is the home of Coca-Cola?

 Natural World
What holiday islands' former name translates as The Fortunate Islands?

 History
Which Scottish king killed Duncan and was himself killed by Duncan's son Malcolm?

 Culture & Belief
In what country have half a million Christians been killed for their beliefs since 1975?

 Stage & Screen
What kind of car was Disney's Love Bug?

 Written Word
What, according to Lady Macbeth, would not sweeten her little hand?

 Music
Who gave up his seat to the Big Bopper, on the plane that killed him?

 Famous People
Nicholas Breakspear is the only Englishman to become what?

 Sport & Leisure
In modern fencing, the swords used are the sabre, epeé and which other?

 Science & Tech
What planet does the moon Ganymede belong to?

 True or False?
Mars Bars were created by a Mr Mars; true or false?

ANSWERS: PAGE 147

Food & Drink
Pepsi is so called because it was said to cure which ailment?

 Natural World
What is the more common term for dyspepsia?

 History
Which seafaring leader began life right-handed and ended it left-handed?

 Culture & Belief
What is the English translation of Descartes' maxim 'Cogito, ergo sum'?

 Stage & Screen
What actor said in a film 'A man's gotta do what a man's gotta do'?

 Written Word
What were the magic words that opened the doors of the Forty Thieves' treasure cave?

 Music
Who said to a royal variety show audience 'Those in the cheap seats clap, the rest rattle your jewellery'?

 Famous People
What ageing Lothario did Shirley Maclaine say was age 50 from the neck up and 14 from the waist down?

 Sport & Leisure
Why is Bob Charles unique among winners of golf majors?

 Science & Tech
How many moons has the planet Saturn – 8, 12, 18 or 25?

 True or False?
English is the world's most widely spoken language; true or false?

Food & Drink

Fred the flour grader is the trademark of which company?

Natural World

What plant is saffron a product of?

History

In 1752 the Julian calendar was replaced by what?

Culture & Belief

What month in our calendar is called after a Roman emperor?

Stage & Screen

What horror classic promised to pay £10,000 to the first cinema-goer who died of fright watching it?

Written Word

What poor woodcutter discovered the magic words to open the treasure cave of the Forty Thieves?

Music

What record did *Pulp Fiction*'s Vincent and Mia dance to in the twist contest at Jackrabbit Slim's?

Famous People

What US actress was made a French Chevalier of Arts in 1995 in recognition of her film work?

Sport & Leisure

What 20th-century golfing genius retired aged 28, having already won the Grand Slam?

Science & Tech

How many degrees from the Greenwich meridian is the international date line?

True or False?

The Hundred Years War did not last a hundred years; true or false?

ANSWERS: PAGE 148

Food & Drink
What substance is the basic ingredient of mead?

Natural World
How many degrees of the earth's surface does the sun pass over in an hour?

History
Which English king did Robert the Bruce defeat at Bannockburn?

Culture & Belief
What Christian celebration is Advent a time of preparation for?

Stage & Screen
What was Dirty Harry's surname?

Written Word
Who wrote the *Foundation* trilogy of sci-fi novels?

Music
The Flowers of the Forest is a lament for the dead of which battle between England and Scotland?

Famous People
What religion is Richard Gere a follower of?

Sport & Leisure
What was the score in the first ever football international, between Scotland and England?

Science & Tech
What comet is thought to have been seen as the Star of Bethlehem, foretelling the birth of Christ?

True or False?
Music to be played at 'allegro tempo' would be played at a very slow speed; true or false?

ANSWERS: PAGE 149

Food & Drink

How many fluid ounces are there in a pint?

Natural World

What is Mount Godwin-Austen in the Himalayas more commonly known as?

History

Who led the peasants' revolt in the 14th century?

Culture & Belief

What Old Testament leader was prepared to sacrifice his son to God?

Stage & Screen

What did the films *The Odd Couple*, *MASH* and *Nine To Five* have in common?

Written Word

Which Brontë sister wrote *Wuthering Heights*?

Music

Who wrote the *1812 Overture*?

Famous People

Which stars took out a high-profile ad in *The Times* to declare their love 2 months before filing for divorce?

Sport & Leisure

In bowls, how does a crown green differ from a level green?

Science & Tech

To the nearest five years, how often does Halley's Comet return?

True or False?

Nancy Astor was the first woman to address the House of Commons; true or false?

ANSWERS: PAGE 149

Food & Drink
What gives pesto sauce its colour?

Natural World
What is the most northerly line of latitude where the sun can be directly overhead?

History
Who was king of England when Wat Tyler led the peasants' revolt?

Culture & Belief
A person born on 2 September would be which zodiac sign?

Stage & Screen
What was the registration number of Lady Penelope's Rolls Royce in *Thunderbirds*?

Written Word
What arts critic adapted his own novel *A Time to Dance* for TV?

Music
What melancholy name did Tchaikovsky give to his sixth and final symphony?

Famous People
Who is the richest businessman in the world?

Sport & Leisure
What type of sportsman would use a grinner, a palomar and a half-blood?

Science & Tech
In computer terminology, what does DOS stand for?

True or False?
Noah's ark came to rest on Mount Sinai; true or false?

ANSWERS: PAGE 150

Food & Drink
What is the main ingredient of egg noodles?

 Natural World
What kind of creature is a miller's dog?

 History
Which real-life killer first came to the big screen in Alfred Hitchcock's 1926 film *The Lodger*?

 Culture & Belief
The Four Horsemen of the Apocalypse rode different-coloured horses; who rode the pale horse?

 Stage & Screen
What is the connection between Kermit the Frog and *Star Wars* Jedi master Yoda?

 Written Word
How did Scarlett O'Hara and Rhett Butler's daughter die?

 Music
Which two singers died within weeks of recording TV shows with David Bowie?

 Famous People
Who played the part of Muhammad Ali in the bio-pic of his life, *The Greatest*?

 Sport & Leisure
Who regained the World Heavyweight Boxing championship twice?

 Science & Tech
What nickname was given to Ronald Reagan's Strategic Defence Initiative?

 True or False?
Alfred Hitchcock was born in Singapore; true or false?

ANSWERS: PAGE 150

Food & Drink

If herbs are the green parts of plants, what are spices?

Natural World

Who was the first recorded man to cross the Antarctic circle?

History

Which country was split by the 38th Parallel?

Culture & Belief

What do British magicians call their professional ruling body?

Stage & Screen

Fleegle, Bingo, Drooper and Snorky were a bunch of hairy TV pop stars collectively known as what?

Written Word

Which TV critic on *The Observer* newspaper wrote the novels *Metroland* and *Flaubert's Parrot*?

Music

What was the name of the Spice Girls' film?

Famous People

Which two Africans were joint winners of the 1993 Nobel Peace Prize?

Sport & Leisure

What two international cricketing sides met for the first time ever in 1877?

Science & Tech

How long in hours will a colour TV run on one unit of electricity?

True or False?

Madonna's real first name is Mary; true or false?

Food & Drink The goddess of the harvest gives her name to which staple food?

 Natural World Captain Cook was murdered in which island group?

 History Shirley Williams and David Owen were two of the SDP gang of four. Who were the other two?

 Culture & Belief The Greek and Roman god of the sun shared the same name; what was it?

 Stage & Screen What film featured Bill Murray as a weatherman forced to live the same day over and over again?

 Written Word *In Down with Skool,* who describes poetry as 'sissy stuff that rhymes'?

 Music Who asked you to *Sound Your Funky Horn* and *Shake Your Booty*?

 Famous People Which '90s artist displayed various animals in tanks of formaldehyde?

 Sport & Leisure Irrespective of which country holds them, where are 'the Ashes' on display?

 Science & Tech Who invented the mercury thermometer?

 True or False? *The Sun* sells more copies each day than all the quality broadsheets combined; true or false?

ANSWERS: PAGE 151

Food & Drink
On average, what do we consume two teaspoons of, every day?

 Natural World
What American state's nickname is The Last Frontier?

 History
What were the Women's Social and Political Union better known as?

 Culture & Belief
What German word describes the spirit of the age?

 Stage & Screen
Who was Edmund Blackadder's sidekick through the ages?

 Written Word
How many letters are there in the Greek alphabet?

 Music
Which British actress/comedienne said 'All I want for Christmas is a Beatle'?

 Famous People
Who was the first Tudor queen of England?

 Sport & Leisure
What German football hero was nicknamed The Kaiser?

 Science & Tech
Eiffel Tower designer Gustave Eiffel also designed locks for which canal?

 True or False?
The Sun has the biggest daily circulation of any English-language newspaper in the world; true or false?

ANSWERS: PAGE 152

Food & Drink What is the trademark of Bacardi?

 Natural World Name three of the original Cinque Ports on England's south coast.

 History Who founded the Suffragettes in 1903?

 Culture & Belief Whose title is Mikado?

 Stage & Screen What famous film series was Gerald Thomas responsible for?

 Written Word Who was chuffed at pulling Annie and Clarabel?

 Music The D'oyly Carte opera company is most associated with whose light operas?

 Famous People Mrs Bandaranaike, the world's first woman prime minister, was premier of which country?

 Sport & Leisure Hawaiian Sunny Garcia is a leading exponent of which sport?

 Science & Tech What did Karl Benz name after his daughter?

 True or False? Batman appeared on TV before Superman; true or false?

ANSWERS: PAGE 152

Food & Drink

What procedure removes the the threat of brucellosis from milk?

Natural World

Which organ of the body contains insulin?

History

Who was elected president of the Philippines after people power ousted Marcos?

Culture & Belief

Where would an American put a diaper?

Stage & Screen

What classic film series featured the characters W. C. Boggs, D. S. Bung and the Khasi of Kalabar?

Written Word

What island are the *Thomas the Tank Engine* stories set on?

Music

Who wrote the songs for Beatles take-off band the Rutles?

Famous People

In 1953, what Nobel Prize did Winston Churchill win?

Sport & Leisure

The term 'pegging out' has come to mean dying, but means finishing which sport?

Science & Tech

In 1903 Antoine Becquerel shared the Nobel Prize for Physics with which married couple?

True or False?

The founder of the Nobel Peace Prize was also the inventor of dynamite; true or false?

ANSWERS: PAGE 153

Food & Drink
What is a prune?

 Natural World
Which famous port is on the Hawaiian island of Oahu?

 History
Which simple box camera was designed for Kodak by Frank Brownell?

 Culture & Belief
If you had a fender-bender in the US, what would have happened?

 Stage & Screen
What 1960s British comedy film was subtitled *The British position in India*?

 Written Word
What one-time silent-film star was the first actor ever to appear on the cover of *Time* magazine?

 Music
What was the Beatles' first film?

 Famous People
Clement Attlee's biography was called *As It Happened*, but whose was called *As It Happens*?

 Sport & Leisure
What sport would you use a malibu board for?

 Science & Tech
Name one of the companies which developed CDs.

True or False?
Brownsville, Texas, is the hottest city in the USA; true or false?

ANSWERS: PAGE 153

Food & Drink Which sugar features the trademark Mr Cube?

 Natural World What substance is stored in the gall bladder?

 History Who has controlled Gibraltar for the longest period, Britain or Spain?

 Culture & Belief How would you be feeling if you were tristful?

 Stage & Screen What colour is Po Tellytubby?

 Written Word What Shakespeare play was the basis for the musical *Kiss Me Kate*?

 Music Who was a '70s chart-topper with *Can the Can, 48 Crash* and *Devil Gate Drive*?

 Famous People Who was the self-styled Chairman of the Board of the Rat Pack?

 Sport & Leisure Which British skater won an Olympic gold in 1976?

 Science & Tech Which two sugar magnates never met?

 True or False? The blackbird is Britain's commonest bird; true or false?

ANSWERS: PAGE 154

Food & Drink

Which two fruits are crossed to make ugli fruit?

Natural World

What is the modern-day name of the sea that pirates used to call the Spanish Main?

History

Who was England's last reigning Tudor monarch?

Culture & Belief

What is the collective term for a group of leopards?

Stage & Screen

Who played Vito Corleone in *The Godfather Part II*?

Written Word

What book by Harper Lee, later made into a film, features the character Boo Radley?

Music

What film was the chart-topping tune *Duelling Banjos* taken from?

Famous People

Which two poets' love affair was chronicled in the film *The Barretts of Wimpole Street*?

Sport & Leisure

Where was the 1970 World Cup played?

Science & Tech

What does EMI stand for?

True or False?

India produces more films each year than the USA; true or false?

ANSWERS: PAGE 154

Food &
Drink
What is the literal translation of the German dish sauerkraut?

Natural
World
What is the largest mammal in the world?

History
Who was Britain's last reigning Stuart monarch?

Culture &
Belief
Which of the 12 Apostles is the patron saint of tax officials?

Stage &
Screen
What comedy series' central character is a Seattle-based radio psychiatrist?

Written
Word
Shakespeare's Romeo and Juliet became Tony and Maria in what Broadway smash hit musical?

Music
Who wrote the musical *Blood Brothers*?

Famous
People
Who was Elizabeth I's mother?

Sport &
Leisure
The St Andrew's Club was founded during the reign of which golf-playing queen?

Science
& Tech
What killer disease was officially declared eradicated by the World Health Organisation in 1980?

True or
False?
Iceland's President Finnbogadottir, elected in 1980, was the world's first elected female head of state; true or false?

ANSWERS: PAGE 155

Food & Drink   In America a health warning on bottles and cans advises who not to drink alcohol?

 Natural World   Where is the Napa Valley wine-producing area?

 History   What late-19th century craft movement was the designer William Morris particularly associated with?

 Culture & Belief   What is Sianel Pedwar Cymru more commonly known as?

 Stage & Screen   What is Frasier's second name?

 Written Word   In the Mario Puzo novel, what is the name of *The Godfather*?

 Music   What was the name of the only movie the Monkees ever made?

 Famous People   Which of the services did James Stewart and Clark Gable join in the Second World War?

 Sport & Leisure   What 1976 Olympic gymnast was the first ever to achieve a perfect score?

 Science & Tech   What type of doctors specialise in the care of pregnant women and unborn babies?

 True or False?   The English are the world's greatest beer consumers; true or false?

ANSWERS: PAGE 155

Food & Drink
If a Scotsman is eating champit neeps, what is on his plate?

Natural World
Salmon fishing and whisky distilling are associated with a particular Scottish river; what is it?

History
What area was brought under British control by the Opium War?

Culture & Belief
What is the newspaper of the Salvation Army?

Stage & Screen
What classic TV series featured two brothers called Little Joe and Hoss?

Written Word
What is the full name of Major Major in *Catch 22*?

Music
What '90s stage hit is based on Puccini's opera *Madam Butterfly*?

Famous People
Which pop star took lead roles in *Ned Kelly*, *Performance* and *Freejack*?

Sport & Leisure
What shape is the field where a baseball match is played?

Science & Tech
On the Mohs hardness scale, what is the hardest mineral?

True or False?
Hong Kong has more skyscrapers than New York; true or false?

ANSWERS: PAGE 156

Food & Drink How many teaspoons of sugar are there in one packet jelly?

 Natural World What is Holy Island, off England's north-east coast, also known as?

 History Which type of aeroplanes competed for the Schneider Trophy?

 Culture & Belief Where would you expect to see a Mexican Wave?

 Stage & Screen Who spent years fighting the Autons, Silurians, Sea Devils and Drashigs?

 Written Word In what branch of business are Booker Prize sponsors Booker McConnel company?

 Music The Rogers and Hammerstein musical *Carousel* was the source of what famous football anthem?

 Famous People Where was Labour leader John Smith buried?

 Sport & Leisure How many men make up a baseball team?

 Science & Tech Which two stations are connected by the Glasgow to London west coast rail line?

True or False? The most common surname in both Britain and the USA is Smith; true or false?

ANSWERS: PAGE 156

Food & Drink
UHT milk lasts indefinitely if unopened. What does UHT stand for?

Natural World
What is the only internal human organ that can reproduce itself?

History
In what year did Britain have three kings?

Culture & Belief
What help was Simon of Cyrene supposed to have given Jesus?

Stage & Screen
How many of the Magnificent Seven are left alive at the end of the film?

Written Word
In 1516, Sir Thomas More first used which name for an ideal society?

Music
What hit did Bill Haley change the lyrics of to avoid anything suggestive?

Famous People
Which sea captain was set adrift by his crew and later became governor of New South Wales?

Sport & Leisure
What player claimed the hand of God helped him score a goal in the 1986 World Cup?

Science & Tech
If diamond is rated 10 on the Mohs hardness scale, what is the rating of talc?

True or False?
Bill Haley and the Comets were the first American group to have a number 1 hit in the UK; true or false?

ANSWERS: PAGE 157

Food & Drink
Vegetarians will not eat cheese containing which animal derivative?

Natural World
How do frogs breathe while underwater?

History
How was Kublai Khan related to Genghis Khan?

Culture & Belief
What is the name for the 14 books of the Bible that appear in Catholic but not in Protestant versions?

Stage & Screen
What long-running kids' TV show began in 1958 fronted by Christopher Trace and Leila Williams?

Written Word
Who wrote *Slaugherhouse 5*?

Music
Rock Around the Clock was a hit after it featured in which film?

Famous People
Which warrior lived longest: Alexander the Great, Genghis Khan or Attila the Hun?

Sport & Leisure
What was unusual about the 1912 Boat Race?

Science & Tech
Where in the US did the Wright brothers make the first controlled flight?

True or False?
Wilbur Wright was the first man to fly in a heavier-than-air aircraft; true or false?

ANSWERS: PAGE 157

Food & Drink If an egg floats on water, is it fresh or stale?

 Natural World Apart from lying down, what can fish not do as they sleep?

 History When was the United Nations charter signed, in San Francisco?

 Culture & Belief What was The Sweeney cockney rhyming slang for?

 Stage & Screen What cult TV detective series saw Bruce Willis first make his name?

 Written Word Where in Aberdeenshire was Robert Louis Stevenson living when he wrote *Treasure Island*?

 Music Who played the role of Jim Morrison in the 1991 film *The Doors*?

 Famous People Which battle was Nelson's last?

 Sport & Leisure What footballing first did Stanley Matthews achieve in 1965?

 Science & Tech What did Charles Lindbergh call his Atlantic-crossing plane?

 True or False? On the *Bounty*, William Bligh actually held the rank of lieutenant; true or false?

ANSWERS: PAGE 158

What is the best grain for making beer?

What is the world's largest island?

Who was the first US president to appear on TV?

What day every year does New Orleans' famous Mardi Gras festival take place on?

What cult '60s show featured agents of the United Network Command for Law and Enforcement?

What character in *Don Quixote* was called Rosinante?

Which is made of wood – glockenspiel or xylophone?

How is author Charles Dodgson better known?

Who rode Nijinsky to win the Derby in 1970?

What pain-killer is derived from the bark of the willow tree?

In Scrabble, 'Q' is worth 12 points; true or false?

ANSWERS: PAGE 158

Food & Drink
What is the French term used for a bundle or bag of herbs?

Natural World
What is the world's most sparsely populated country?

History
What was the name of Britain's first Polaris submarine?

Culture & Belief
Which month starts with All Saints' Day?

Stage & Screen
What do TV shows *The Man From UNCLE, Sapphire and Steel* and *The Invisible Man* have in common?

Written Word
Who won Pulitzer Prizes for *Rabbit is Rich* in 1982 and *Rabbit at Rest* in 1991?

Music
What chart-topping music was the theme to the terrifying 1973 film *The Exorcist*?

Famous People
Charles Dodgson, better known as Lewis Carroll, lectured in which subject at Oxford?

Sport & Leisure
In what year was the Grand National declared void?

Science & Tech
What was the frankencycle?

True or False?
Iceland is the country nearest to the North Pole; true or false?

ANSWERS: PAGE 159

Food & Drink

What is the Italian name for corn meal?

Natural World

What is the world's most densely populated country?

History

Which decade saw Switzerland give its women the vote in national elections?

Culture & Belief

In which month is All Souls' Day?

Stage & Screen

What coveted object did Bob Hope describe as 'a bookend with a sneer'?

Written Word

The memorial to Lewis Carroll in Llandudno is a statue of what?

Music

Who co-wrote *Mull of Kintyre* with Paul McCartney but sold his rights after being declared bankrupt?

Famous People

What celebrity father and daughter duo appeared together in the award-winning film *Paper Moon*?

Sport & Leisure

In croquet, if your balls are black and blue, what colour are your opponent's balls?

Science & Tech

What letter lies to the right of Y on a QWERTY keyboard?

True or False?

Agatha Christie is the most-translated author in the world; true or false?

ANSWERS: PAGE 159

What kind of fruit is a Cox's Orange Pippin?

 What American state is Carson City the capital of?

 When was the last execution at the Tower of London (to the nearest 10 years)?

 The work of art called *La Gioconda* is better known as what?

 How many Oscars did *Brief Encounter, Rebel Without A Cause* and *Psycho* win between them?

 Whiat Michael Ondaatje story won the Booker Prize in 1992 and the best picture Oscar in 1997?

 What adjective is usually used to describe rock 'n' roller Richard Penniman?

 Who was the first actor to refuse an Oscar award?

 Which is larger, a croquet lawn or a tennis court?

 What 1982 film was computer animation first used in?

True or False? Humphrey Bogart won only one Oscar; true or false?

ANSWERS: PAGE 160

Food & Drink
Which biscuit is named after an Italian soldier?

Natural World
What Hebridean island is Fingal's Cave on?

History
What state saw the last executions for witchcraft in the USA?

Culture & Belief
What ancient Celtic festival marks the old year's end with a driving away of the spirits of the newly dead?

Stage & Screen
What instrument does Lisa Simpson play?

Written Word
What book won Salman Rushdie the Booker Prize in 1981?

Music
What band did Frank Sinatra sing with before going solo?

Famous People
What more light-footed name was Frederick Austerlitz better known as?

Sport & Leisure
Which two teams have football grounds called the Stadium of Light?

Science & Tech
Which lightweight metal is made from bauxite?

True or False?
Sharp-shooter Annie Oakley once shot a cigarette from between the lips of Kaiser Wilhelm; true or false?

ANSWERS: PAGE 160

Food & Drink What name is given to a pudding with pears, and very thin toast?

 Natural World What colour is amethyst?

 History Where was the investiture of Prince Charles as Prince of Wales?

 Culture & Belief In Greek mythology what did Prometheus steal from Olympus?

 Stage & Screen *Welcome to Berlin* was the original title of what famous stage show?

 Written Word In Samuel Beckett's most famous play, what are Vladimir and Estragon doing?

 Music Which soul singer fronted a band called Grand Central, with Prince on guitar?

 Famous People What did *The New York Herald* sponsor Henry Stanley's expedition to do in Africa?

 Sport & Leisure What film saw footballer John Wark appear alongside actor Sylvester Stallone?

 Science & Tech Which aid to navigation is called, in full, radio detection and ranging?

 True or False? Gordon Bennett was a real person and was the newspaper proprietor who sent Stanley to Africa to look for Dr Livingstone; true or false?

ANSWERS: PAGE 161

Food & Drink

What kind of fruit are Green Williams?

Natural World

What is the longest mountain range on earth?

History

How many presidents has the USA had, including Bill Clinton?

Culture & Belief

In the language of flowers, what does rosemary represent?

Stage & Screen

Who originally played Sally Bowles in the 1968 London stage version of *Cabaret*?

Written Word

Edith, Osbert and Sachaverell were members of what literary family?

Music

Which of Holst's *Planet Suite* depicts the bringer of jollity?

Famous People

Which US president took the decision to drop the first atomic bomb?

Sport & Leisure

Which yacht racing cup was originally called the Queen's Cup?

Science & Tech

Which is the Third Rock From The Sun?

True or False?

Bill Clinton is taller than Abraham Lincoln was; true or false?

ANSWERS: PAGE 161

Food & Drink
What method of cooking might an American call broiling?

Natural World
What is the world's biggest country?

History
Of the 42 presidents of the USA, how many have been Republicans?

Culture & Belief
Which British coin has a portcullis on the reverse?

Stage & Screen
What musical starred Richard Gere in its London stage version and John Travolta in its film?

Written Word
What novel by nine-year-old Daisy Ashford was published with her mis-spellings intact?

Music
Which new wave band featured guitarist Luke Warm, sax player William Mysterious, and singer Fay Fife?

Famous People
What country was the dancer Dame Ninette de Valois born in?

Sport & Leisure
Name two cities to have hosted more than one Olympic Games.

Science & Tech
What is a one thousand millionth of a second called?

True or False?
Gerald Ford was never elected to the post of either president or vice-president of the US; true or false?

ANSWERS: PAGE 162

Food & Drink
What kind of fruit is an Elegant Lady?

 Natural World
What fruit was the cargo of the *Bounty* when the crew mutinied?

 History
In what year was the Domesday Book compiled?

 Culture & Belief
What is the first commandment?

 Stage & Screen
Anthony Hopkins, Charles Laughton and Lon Chaney all played a love-sick campanologist; who was he?

 Written Word
A map of what island shows Foremast Hill, Spyglass Hill and Mizzenmast Hill?

 Music
What 1970s band dropped Guildford from their original name?

 Famous People
What famous American family was '60s actor and Rat Pack member Peter Lawford married into?

 Sport & Leisure
How many eyes can be seen on a deck of cards?

 Science & Tech
A year of which planet is equal to 84 earth years?

 True or False?
Ombrophobia is the fear of umbrellas; true or false?

ANSWERS: PAGE 162

Food & Drink
What is a Pink Lady?

 Natural World
In what century was the last living dodo sighted?

 History
In what battle did Henry V defeat the French in 1415?

 Culture & Belief
In the song, how many presents were handed over on the 12th day of Christmas?

 Stage & Screen
What was the most enduring and coveted creation of MGM art director Cedric Gibbons?

 Written Word
The title of the war novel *Fair Stood the Wind for France* originally referred to what medieval battle?

 Music
Which rock singer/producer wrote the words for the Lloyd Webber musical *Whistle Down the Wind*?

 Famous People
Explorer Henry Stanley fought in the American Civil War. On which side?

 Sport & Leisure
What is the penalty if a show jumper falls off their horse?

 Science & Tech
What chemical element has the atomic number one?

 True or False?
John F. Kennedy features on the back of the US $50 bill; true or false?

ANSWERS: PAGE 163

Food & Drink Does a cheesecake contain cheese?

Natural World What is the modern name for Byzantium?

History The Union Jack combines the flags of which three saints?

Culture & Belief How many days after St David's day is St Patrick's day?

Stage & Screen Where does the action in *Zorba the Greek* actually take place?

Written Word What Irish writer's novel, *Murphy*, did Dylan Thomas describe as 'Sodom and Begorrah'?

Music Which American composer wrote *Alexander's Rag Time Band* and *Annie Get Your Gun*?

Famous People What revoluntionary's real name was Vladimir Ilyich Ulyanov?

Sport & Leisure Who were the losing side in the first World Cup final in 1930?

Science & Tech What unlikely material was the bodywork of the East German Trabant car made from?

True or False? Chromophobia is the fear of colour; true or false?

Food & Drink
What type of food can be classed as beef, cherry or plum?

Natural World
What is ferrous oxide commonly known as?

History
Which British king was known as Farmer George?

Culture & Belief
What year would be written MCMLXXXIV in Roman numerals?

Stage & Screen
In what Lloyd-Webber musical would you find Rum Tum Tigger, Mungojerrie and Asparagus?

Written Word
Which poet laureate wrote about the religious troubles of his teddy bear?

Music
What instrument would you associate with Julian Lloyd Webber?

Famous People
How did Anne Boleyn die?

Sport & Leisure
Which sport was invented in a Massachusetts YMCA?

Science & Tech
Which housewives' convenience product was invented by Earl Tupper?

True or False?
The Statue of Liberty stands on Ellis Island at New York harbour; true or false?

ANSWERS: PAGE 164

Food & Drink
What term describes spooning hot fat over a roast?

Natural World
Which island was known as Van Diemon's island?

History
Which two-piece item of clothing is named after an atomic bomb test site?

Culture & Belief
The Watchtower is the magazine of which religious body?

Stage & Screen
Who are the only two characters with names in the stage musical *Godspell*?

Written Word
Who wrote children's poetry in *The Bad Child's Book of Beasts* and *More Beasts for Worse Children*?

Music
Dvorak's *New World Symphony* has become knows as the tune from which adverts?

Famous People
Richard Block and David Quayle founded which DIY chain?

Sport & Leisure
What is the name of the Chicago basketball team?

Science & Tech
Which household convenience was invented by Sir John Harrington?

True or False?
The modern flush toilet was developed by a Mr Crapper; true or false?

ANSWERS: PAGE 164

Food & Drink
On the EC scale for egg sizes 1–7, is 1 the smallest or largest?

Natural World
Which owl is also known as a screech owl?

History
Which ship sank off Cape Race in 1912?

Culture & Belief
What is St Vitus the patron saint of?

Stage & Screen
What valour award does David Jason's fictional detective Frost hold?

Written Word
Which fictional detective stayed in the same street as Holmes and Watson?

Music
What girl's name is the title of Chuck Berry's first hit?

Famous People
How is Prince Philip related to Queen Victoria?

Sport & Leisure
Which Australian won the men's tennis Grand Slam twice in the 1960s?

Science & Tech
Which two planets do not have moons?

True or False?
The USA has a longer frontier than Russia; true or false?

ANSWERS: PAGE 165

Food & Drink

What food might come as a Coburg, Huffkin or Bloomer?

Natural World

Which is the last US state listed alphabetically?

History

How many days was Edward VIII king for?

Culture & Belief

According to the Bible, who shall inherit the earth?

Stage & Screen

What 1998 smash-hit movie was the first successful film spin-off of a current TV series?

Written Word

What nationality is best-selling travel writer Bill Bryson?

Music

Which member of the Beatles was not in the Quarrymen?

Famous People

William Friese-Greene was a pioneer of which popular entertainment?

Sport & Leisure

Who won a record seven gold medals at one Olympic Games in 1972?

Science & Tech

What are the three primary colours which make up television images?

True or False?

New York was named after James, Duke of York, brother of Charles II; true or false?

ANSWERS: PAGE 165

Food & Drink
When might you eat a simnel cake?

 Natural World
Which rivers run through Dublin and Cardiff?

 History
Which was the first industry to be nationalized in post-war Britiain?

 Culture & Belief
What does the phrase 'fiat lux' mean?

 Stage & Screen
Martin Shaw, Ben Kingsley and Joanna Lumley all appeared in what long-running TV series?

 Written Word
Which cult Scottish author adds a middle initial 'M' to his name on his science fiction novels?

 Music
Which little boy did the Coasters sing about, asking *Why's everybody always pickin' on me?*?

Famous People
Which modern-day politician once famously declared that there was no such thing as society?

Sport & Leisure
What two winter sports make up the biathlon?

Science & Tech
What is hi-fi abbreviated from?

True or False?
Britain's greatest sailor, Admiral Nelson suffered terribly from seasickness; true or false?

ANSWERS: PAGE 166

Food & Drink
How many calories, to the nearest 10, are in a glass of sweet white wine?

Natural World
What term describes a warm spell of weather in late autumn?

History
The Iran-Contra affair provided guns to fight which Nicaraguan regime?

Culture & Belief
Martin Luther nailed his 95 Theses to the Wittenburg church door in which century?

Stage & Screen
Mr Ed talked his way to stardom in the eponymous 1960s TV show. What was unusual about him?

Written Word
What did Oscar Wilde describe as 'the unspeakable in full pursuit of the uneatable'?

Music
Who did Stevie Wonder sing *Happy Birthday* to in his 1982 single?

Famous People
Who was assassinated at Memphis, Tennessee in 1968?

Sport & Leisure
1,000 Guineas; 2,000 Guineas; The Oaks; The Derby. Name the missing classic horse race.

Science & Tech
What unit of engines' power is equal to 745 watts?

True or False?
New York was home to the world's first skyscraper; true or false?

ANSWERS: PAGE 166

Food & Drink
How many minutes of housework are required to burn off the calories in a 25g bag of crisps?

Natural World
The Menai Bridge links mainland Wales and which island?

History
The rationing of what ended on 15 March 1949?

Culture & Belief
How did French economist Proudhon answer his own question 'What is property?'

Stage & Screen
What US comedy show started the careers of stars like Dan Aykroyd, Eddie Murphy and Billy Crystal?

Written Word
Author John Buchan became Governor-general of what Commonwealth country?

Music
Who starred as Pink in the film version of *The Wall*?

Famous People
Newspaper owner and politician Lord Beaverbrook was born in which country?

Sport & Leisure
Who has won most motor racing World Championships?

Science & Tech
Where in a building would you find headers, stretchers, halfbats and queen closers?

True or False?
A cummerbund is worn around the head; true or false?

ANSWERS: PAGE 167

Which has most protein per 100g, baked beans, peanuts or cheddar cheese?

 Which three US states start with the letter O?

 Whose 1950s economic programme was called The Great Leap Forward?

 How many different portraits of Queen Elizabeth II have appeared on British coins?

 What colourful children's TV classic opens to the tune of *Barnacle Bill*?

 Which newspaper did Lord Beaverbrook say he ran for no other purpose than propaganda?

 Which comic actor had top 10 hits with *Hole in the Ground* and *Right Said Fred*?

 Who succeeded Khrushchev as First Secretary of the Soviet Communist Party?

 Who did Virginia Wade beat in the 1977 Wimbledon singles final?

 Igor Sikorsky designed the first successful version of which method of transport?

 The Union Jack flies at the front of a ship; true or false?

ANSWERS: PAGE 167

Food & Drink
In the names of beers, what do the amounts 60 Shilling, 70 Shilling and 80 Shilling represent?

Natural World
Which channel divides Wales from Ireland?

History
What was the name given to Ronald Reagan's economic policies?

Culture & Belief
In Rome, the goddess of wisdom was Minerva. Who was her Greek counterpart?

Stage & Screen
What was Dr Who's Time And Relative Dimensions In Space machine better known as?

Written Word
What was the first thing Kingsley Amis said he would buy with his Booker Prize?

Music
Whose book was called *The One Who Writes the Words for Elton John*?

Famous People
How did cosmonaut Yuri Gagarin die?

Sport & Leisure
Which sport features the Sugar Bowl, Rose Bowl and Cotton Bowl?

Science & Tech
Where might you normally see the Welsh phrase 'Pleidiol wyf im gwlad'?

True or False?
Israel has the largest Jewish population in the world; true or false?

Food & Drink — What pastry is used to make chocolate eclairs?

Natural World — What colour is the flower of a marigold?

History — How many British monarchs have there been since 1900?

Culture & Belief — How is the Society of Friends more commonly known?

Stage & Screen — Name three of the *Roads* that Bing Crosby and Bob Hope took?

Written Word — Charles Bukovski wrote the screen play for which film starring Faye Dunnaway and Mickey Rourke?

Music — Who were the three members of the Jam?

Famous People — Which director supposedly inspired Ed Wood to pursue his film career?

Sport & Leisure — What nationality were motor racing champions Piquet, Senna and Fittipaldi?

Science & Tech — How many sides does a 20p coin have?

True or False? — The lion is the most-mentioned animal in the Bible; true or false?

ANSWERS: PAGE 168

Food & Drink
Kedgeree is made with rice and which other main ingredient?

Natural World
The dappled-sky appearance of alto-cumulus clouds is often likened to which fish?

History
Where are the Tamil Tigers a militant separatist group?

Culture & Belief
How is Hindu Prince Siddharta Galltama better known?

Stage & Screen
How much did it cost to see a nickelodeon film?

Written Word
What bespectacled boy-wizard is a pupil at Hogwarts School of Witchcraft and Wizardry?

Music
Which *Eastenders* actor reached the top 10 in 1975 with *The Ugly Duckling*?

Famous People
What famous Danish storyteller wrote *The Ugly Duckling*?

Sport & Leisure
Whose ears did Mike Tyson bite during a fight?

Science & Tech
Which number appears on the top right of a push button phone?

True or False?
Images of St Peter normally depict the saint holding a fishing net; true or false?

ANSWERS: PAGE 169

Food & Drink
What colour is saffron?

Natural World
What colour is malachite?

History
Which two airlines merged to become British Airways?

Culture & Belief
How would a newly-minted 2p coin differ from the original 2p coins?

Stage & Screen
What palace did the BBC originally broadcast its TV programmes from?

Written Word
In Scrabble, which letters are worth 8 points?

Music
Which is the deepest-toned bass instrument?

Famous People
How did Blondin cross Niagara Falls?

Sport & Leisure
Which sportswear company is the brand with the three stripes?

Science & Tech
What type of bridge is the Forth Road Bridge?

True or False?
In Venezuela, pink envelopes are charged half the usual postage; true or false?

ANSWERS: PAGE 169

Food & Drink
Can you name one of the South American countries where potatoes were first cultivated?

Natural World
Which two countries border on Uruguay?

History
What Latin-American state was ruled by the Somoza dictatorship?

Culture & Belief
What is the church festival celebrated on 6 January, Twelfth Day?

Stage & Screen
Where in a theatre would you find barn doors?

Written Word
Flaubert said 'You can calculate the worth of a man by the number of his ...' what?

Music
Which well-known jazz musician presents the Radio 4 show *I'm Sorry, I Haven't a Clue*?

Famous People
Which performer's real name was Erich Weiss?

Sport & Leisure
Who won the rugby union World Cup in 1987?

Science & Tech
Chester Carbon devised the first of which now common office machine?

True or False?
An ostrich's eye is bigger than its brain; true or false?

ANSWERS: PAGE 170

Food & Drink
What kind of nuts are also known as filberts?

 Natural World
What river is the Isis better known as?

 History
Juan and Eva Peron ruled Argentina from 1946 till when?

 Culture & Belief
What year in the Gregorian calendar is equal to 5760 in the Jewish calendar?

 Stage & Screen
What motel was the setting for a long-running TV soap in the '60s?

 Written Word
Who is the private detective hero of books by Raymond Chandler?

 Music
Harry Chapin sang about a DJ on what radio station?

 Famous People
Who was the tallest president of the USA?

 Sport & Leisure
Where is the German motor racing Grand Prix held?

 Science & Tech
What is the SI unit of electric resistance?

 True or False?
Jerome K. Jerome's middle initial was short for Kevin; true or false?

ANSWERS: PAGE 170

Food & Drink
In an average serving, which commonly eaten food has the highest iron content?

Natural World
What is the southernmost point on the British mainland?

History
Who was the Argentinian military leader at the time of the Falklands War?

Culture & Belief
Which architect said 'A house is a machine for living in'?

Stage & Screen
What street do TV's *Neighbours* live on?

Written Word
What American author was acquitted after he shot dead his wife in a William Tell-style stunt?

Music
What soul pairing duetted on *Endless Love* in 1981?

Famous People
How is architect and designer Charles Edward Jeanneret better known?

Sport & Leisure
What sport would you see at Hickstead?

Science & Tech
In the imperial system, how many gallons were in a peck?

True or False?
Peking was the first city to have a population of a million; true or false?

ANSWERS: PAGE 171

Food & Drink What is the chemical name for vinegar?

 Natural World Which is the largest lake in the USA?

 History In 1984, who was assassinated by her Sikh bodyguards?

 Culture & Belief If the most able rule in a meritocracy, who rule in a gynocracy?

 Stage & Screen Where was Rick's Café?

 Written Word *Babycakes* was the fourth book in what televised series by Armistead Maupin?

 Music How many ways did Paul Simon sing of leaving your lover?

 Famous People Which Greek philosopher argued that since movement exists, there must be a god causing movement?

 Sport & Leisure Which golf major did Arnold Palmer fail to win?

 Science & Tech How many sheets of A4 paper could be cut from one sheet of A0?

 True or False? Cows have two stomachs; true or false?

ANSWERS: PAGE 171

Food & Drink   What is muscovado?

Natural World   How are the Sandwich Islands now known?

History   How was Indira Gandhi related to Mahatma Gandhi?

Culture & Belief   What pet name for a dog is Latin for 'I trust'?

Stage & Screen   What cities did Morse, Taggart and Van der Valk police?

Written Word   Who wrote the lines 'Don't follow leaders, watch parkin' meters'?

Music   What country was the birthplace of Chopin?

Famous People   How did Boadicea die?

Sport & Leisure   When Boris Becker was the first unseeded player to win Wimbledon, who did he beat in the final?

Science & Tech   What method of transport did Christopher Cockerell invent?

True or False?   A rhino's horn is actually made of compacted hair; true or false?

ANSWERS: PAGE 172

Food & Drink — Which pudding comes from the root of the cassava plant?

 Natural World — What constellation are the stars Castor and Pollux in?

 History — How long did the first circumnavigation of the earth via the two poles take?

 Culture & Belief — What do Americans call an apartment with two floors?

 Stage & Screen — What cities are home to the Abbey, Citizens and Crucible theatres?

 Written Word — What historic event took place at midnight in the book *Midnight's Children*?

 Music — Which number was Schubert's Unfinished Symphony?

 Famous People — What did Howard Carter and the Earl of Carnarvon find in 1922?

 Sport & Leisure — What adjective is used to describe Goodwood Racecourse?

 Science & Tech — In 1962, which train made its centenary journey?

 True or False? — The first powered flight by the Wright brothers lasted for 62 seconds; true or false?

ANSWERS: PAGE 172

Food & Drink
Sailors combated which disease with limes for vitamin C?

Natural World
The mistral winds blow from which mountains?

History
In 1971 east Pakistan became which independent nation?

Culture & Belief
Where about your person might you find a hologram of William Shakespeare?

Stage & Screen
Liberty Bell was the signature tune for what completely different comedy show in the 1960s?

Written Word
Which Scottish loch is the setting for Sir Walter Scott's *The Lady of the Lake*?

Music
Which singer had the most hits without ever reaching number 1?

Famous People
Which pioneering biologist sailed across the world on *The Beagle*?

Sport & Leisure
What is the perfect score in ten-pin bowling?

Science & Tech
How would you describe an iron bucket coated in zinc?

True or False?
The actor Nicholas Cage is the nephew of director Francis Ford Coppola; true or false?

ANSWERS: PAGE 173

Food & Drink

What is cous-cous made from?

Natural World

In what general direction do trade winds blow?

History

Who was Indian's first prime minister?

Culture & Belief

Which weekday did the Romans call 'dies jouis' or Jupiter's day?

Stage & Screen

Which animator, now a film director, first came to fame on *Monty Python's Flying Circus*?

Written Word

Which comedian said 'Gee, dat day Ah read a book – some day Ah'm gonna do it again'?

Music

Which song kept Engelbert Humperdinck in the charts for over a year?

Famous People

Lady Emma Hamilton had a daughter, Horatia. Who was the father?

Sport & Leisure

Who was the first British golfer to win the US Masters at Augusta?

Science & Tech

What does an orrery illustrate in model form?

True or False?

One of Germany's brewing laws regulates the diameter of bubbles in lager; true or false?

ANSWERS: PAGE 173

Food & Drink

What Scottish food did Burns call the chieftain of the pudding race?

Natural World

Which is furthest north between Alicante, Majorca and Ibiza?

History

Who was the last viceroy of India?

Culture & Belief

How many pounds does the slang term 'a monkey' mean?

Stage & Screen

Which is the odd one out: Snowy, Roobarb and Felix?

Written Word

What TV host said of his *Unreliable Memoirs* 'nothing is factual except the bits that sound like fiction'?

Music

What word described Lips Inc's town, the Goodies' gibbon and Jasper Carrot's moped?

Famous People

Who was the first Tudor king of England?

Sport & Leisure

Bishen Bedi was a spin bowler, taking 266 test wickets for which country?

Science & Tech

What would astonomers measure in parsecs?

True or False?

Edinburgh has the oldest university in Scotland; true or false?

ANSWERS: PAGE 174

Food & Drink What shape of pasta would you expect if you asked for conchiglie?

 Natural World In which hemisphere is the Amundsen Sea?

 History What are the Netherlands East Indies now known as?

 Culture & Belief Which island parliament is composed of the Upper House and the House of Keys?

 Stage & Screen What '60s kids' TV show, set on an African nature reserve, featured a cross-eyed lion called Clarence?

 Written Word 'Publish and be sued' was the motto of what magazine's former editor?

 Music Which two types of instrument are played in Japanese *noh* drama?

 Famous People Which planet did Sir William Herschel discover in 1781?

 Sport & Leisure What is umpire Dickie Bird's real name?

 Science & Tech Where were the Royal Botanic Gardens founded in 1759?

 True or False? Lenin was the first president of the USSR; true or false?

ANSWERS: PAGE 174

Food & Drink
How long does it take for one unit of alcohol to leave the body?

Natural World
How many stars appear on the state flag of Texas?

History
Who was elected Richard Nixon's vice-president?

Culture & Belief
What country features the chrysanthemum on its imperial crest?

Stage & Screen
What were the wars being fought in *The Green Berets*, *The Blue Max* and *Cross Of Iron*?

Written Word
Whose poems of obituary in *Private Eye* invariably begin: 'So, farewell then...'?

Music
Between July '64 and August '66, how many consecutive number 1s did the Beatles have?

Famous People
Who painted *The Monarch of the Glen* and designed the lions in Trafalgar Square?

Sport & Leisure
The bodyline method of bowling was introduced to combat which Australian?

Science & Tech
Which Scottish railway station is named after a now-closed sewing machine factory?

True or False?
Stirling Moss never won the world motor racing championship; true or false?

ANSWERS: PAGE 175

Food & Drink
Which county is Eccles, home of the cakes, in?

 Natural World
What is the first animal mentioned in English dictionaries?

 History
What was Gorbachev's policy of internal openness called?

 Culture & Belief
Who were the opposing sides in the Battle of Naseby in 1645?

 Stage & Screen
Who played the part of the Sorcerer's Apprentice in Disney's *Fantasia?*

 Written Word
Whose travel book *Notes from a Small Island* was a runaway success in the UK?

 Music
How many years apart were David Bowie's two chart entries with *Space Oddity?*

 Famous People
Which Italian city is the home of Leonardo da Vinci's *Last Supper?*

 Sport & Leisure
Who, in 1978, was the first player to score a century and take eight wickets in a test?

 Science & Tech
Which cotton fabric was originally made at Calicut in India?

 True or False?
Thomas Edison, pioneer of electricity, helped design the electric chair; true or false?

ANSWERS: PAGE 175

Food & Drink

On a bottle of HP sauce, what does HP stand for?

Natural World

What family of fish does the anchovy belong to?

History

When was the Berlin Wall built?

Culture & Belief

In heraldry, what word describes an animal with its front legs raised one above the other?

Stage & Screen

If Clint Eastwood was the Good and Lee van Cleef the Bad, who was the Ugly?

Written Word

What type of books did Winston Churchill think it good for an uneducated man to read?

Music

Who is the only artist to spend more than 1,000 weeks on the UK singles chart?

Famous People

Who was the Republican candidate beaten in the 1960 presidential election by John F. Kennedy?

Sport & Leisure

Which team holds the record for most consecutive wins of cricket's County Championship?

Science & Tech

The first zip fasteners were designed for doing up which items of clothing?

True or False?

Panama hats originated in Panama; true or false?

ANSWERS: PAGE 176

Food & Drink

What would you put in Russian tea instead of milk?

Natural World

What season begins with the vernal equinox?

History

In what year did the Falklands War take place?

Culture & Belief

When did the union of Great Britain and Ireland come into force?

Stage & Screen

What was the relationship between Luke Skywalker and Princess Leia in *Star Wars*?

Written Word

Which character, when asked who made her, replied 'Nobody... I s'pect I just grow'd'?

Music

Who appears on the cover of Roxy Music's *Siren* album?

Famous People

Samuel Pepys' diaries recorded events in which decade?

Sport & Leisure

How does a test match cricketer qualify for the primary club?

Science & Tech

In 1947 an American pilot coined which phrase for unidentified flying objects?

True or False?

Raith Rovers Football Club's home town is Kirkcaldy; true or false?

ANSWERS: PAGE 176

Food & Drink
How much milk does it take to make a pound of cheese?

Natural World
What are the two main metals combined to make bronze?

History
Where did the Americans' abortive invasion of Cuba take place?

Culture & Belief
Until 1836, there were only six universities in Britain: Oxford, Cambridge and which other four?

Stage & Screen
Who originally presented *Juke Box Jury*?

Written Word
Which Shakespeare character says 'But soft! What light through yonder window breaks'?

Music
Who composed the opera *Lakme* and the ballet *Coppelia*?

Famous People
Tony Blair became the fourth post-war Labour prime minister. Who were the other three?

Sport & Leisure
Which cricket side won the first ever County Championship and Sunday League double?

Science & Tech
Which peasant group destroyed machinery which they feared would destroy their livelihood?

True or False?
Buffalo Bill once kicked off a football match in Glasgow; true or false?

ANSWERS: PAGE 177

Food & Drink
What type of flower is the source of vanilla?

Natural World
What river are the Victoria Falls on?

History
What three statesmen met at the peace conference at Yalta in 1945?

Culture & Belief
The silver hallmark of a harp and crown belongs to which city?

Stage & Screen
Which actor played James Bond for only one film?

Written Word
What was Sherlock Holmes' older brother called?

Music
What instrument is associated with Pablo Cassals?

Famous People
What did the 'D' stand for in Franklin D. Roosevelt's name?

Sport & Leisure
What was Sir Len Hutton's two-innings total on his test debut?

Science & Tech
Chirognomy attempts to read the character from which physical feature?

True or False?
Eboracum was the name the Romans give Lincoln; true or false?

ANSWERS: PAGE 177

Food & Drink
What rays are used in the irradiation of food to preserve it?

Natural World
So-called 'mermaids' purses' found on beaches are in fact the egg cases of which fish?

History
What three statesmen met in peace conference at Potsdam in 1945?

Culture & Belief
If a person dies intestate, what have they not done?

Stage & Screen
What city's film festival awards the Golden Bear?

Written Word
What is the better known nickname of Jame Gatz?

Music
What was jazz musician John Birks Gillespie's nickname?

Famous People
Between Gilbert and Sullivan, who wrote the music?

Sport & Leisure
Where is the Gadaffi stadium cricket ground?

Science & Tech
What measure of liquid equals 10lbs weight of distilled water?

True or False?
The source of the River Rhine is in Austria; true or false?

ANSWERS: PAGE 178

Food & Drink
Which spreadable foodstuff was invented during the Franco-Prussian War?

 Natural World
On average, how much urine does an adult pass in 24 hours, to the nearest 100ml?

 History
Who coined the phrase 'the iron curtain' to describe the division between east and west Europe?

 Culture & Belief
Which country is represented in international vehicle registrations by the letter E?

 Stage & Screen
What was Lovejoy's profession?

 Written Word
What was Miss Marple's first name?

 Music
The Stranglers had 96, but the Goombay Dance Band only had 7; of what?

 Famous People
Leo Tolstoy, author of *War and Peace*, fought in what 19th-century war?

 Sport & Leisure
How many balls start a game of snooker?

 Science & Tech
If someone has the intials BDS after their name, what is their profession?

 True or False?
Females have two X chromosomes; true or false?

ANSWERS: PAGE 178

Food & Drink
Which animal's milk is used to make roquefort cheese?

Natural World
In which year did Hillary and Tenzing climb Everest?

History
What line of fortifications did France build to protect its eastern border?

Culture & Belief
What is the modern Polish name for the city of Danzig?

Stage & Screen
What style of film-making was pioneered by John Grierson?

Written Word
James Joyce's *Ulysses* describes a day in the life of what Dublin character?

Music
In *Three Steps to Heaven*, what is step one?

Famous People
Which Irishman founded both a church and political party?

Sport & Leisure
Who were the first two men to win world professional titles at snooker and billiards?

Science & Tech
What does a red fire extinguisher contain?

True or False?
Ireland became a republic in 1922; true or false?

ANSWERS: PAGE 179

Food & Drink
What type of soft cheese was traditionally made from buffaloes' milk?

 Natural World
Who does fratricide involve killing?

 History
What does the name 'Bolsheviks' mean?

 Culture & Belief
If an MBE is a member of the order of the British Empire, what is an OBE?

 Stage & Screen
Where was the first-ever film festival held?

 Written Word
The *Two Towers* is the second book in which trilogy?

 Music
What, according to Ian Dury, is Wee Willie Harris?

 Famous People
Which Italian is celebrated by an American public holiday on 12 October?

 Sport & Leisure
Which three modern-day players have each won the world professional snooker championship 6 times?

 Science & Tech
The members of New York's Diners Club were the first to own what item?

 True or False?
Tony Blair was once the long-haired lead singer with a student rock band; true or false?

ANSWERS: PAGE 179

Food & Drink Which Italian city does parmesan cheese come from?

 Natural World What are Biscay, Trafalgar, Fastnet and German Bight?

 History When did Russia withdraw from the First World War?

 Culture & Belief Which workers can join the ASLEF union?

 Stage & Screen What record-breaking film marked Clint Eastwood's directorial debut?

 Written Word What are Times, Courier and Garamond examples of?

 Music How many quavers make a crotchet?

 Famous People Who is missing from this sequence: Fisher, Ramsay, Coggan, ..., Carey?

 Sport & Leisure What does Len Ganley referee?

 Science & Tech What does SCUBA stand for?

 True or False? Postboxes in Spain are yellow; true or false?

ANSWERS: PAGE 180

Food & Drink
Which crop is threatened by the Colorado beetle?

 Natural World
What river does the Hoover Dam stand on?

 History
What did Captain Robert Jenkins display in London in 1738, leading to a war with Spain?

 Culture & Belief
On the Queen's coat of arms, which country is represented by the unicorn?

 Stage & Screen
What classic 1952 Western was based on a story called *The Tin Badge*?

 Written Word
In which three successive years in the 1950s was *Lord of the Rings* published in three parts?

 Music
What is a violinist's bow string made of?

 Famous People
Which wit declared that 'Nothing succeeds like excess'?

 Sport & Leisure
Who, in 1970, was the first Briton for 50 years to win the US Golf Open?

 Science & Tech
How would the police catch a criminal using dactylography?

True or False?
Sir Walter Raleigh was responsible for introducing the potato to Britain; true or false?

Food & Drink — What are Kerr's Pinks and Maris Pipers?

Natural World — If hens sit on their eggs for three weeks, how long do swans sit on theirs?

History — When were British women given equal voting rights to men?

Culture & Belief — Which 13th-century saint's followers were known as the Grey Friars?

Stage & Screen — Which of his films did Stanley Kubrick withdraw from release after it was criticised?

Written Word — Which American author has written extensively about everyday life in Lake Wobegon?

Music — What colour is common to hits by Fleetwood Mac, The Lemon Pipers and Shakin' Stevens?

Famous People — Which star of the Kirov ballet defected in 1979?

Sport & Leisure — What sport would you play with a mashie?

Science & Tech — Chuck Yeager was the first pilot to break what?

True or False? — All horses have the same official birthday; true or false?

ANSWERS: PAGE 181

Food & Drink — What vegetable is vodka sometimes made from?

 Natural World — Grilse are young of which fish?

 History — The colony at Botany Bay led to the establishment of which city?

 Culture & Belief — What did Jesus do with water in the village of Cana?

 Stage & Screen — What acting first was bestowed on Henry Irving in 1895?

 Written Word — William Donaldson wrote spoof letters to celebrities using what pseudonym?

 Music — What was the avaricious-sounding subtitle of the Pet Shop Boys' hit *Opportunities*?

 Famous People — What did William Wilberforce fight in Parliament to abolish?

 Sport & Leisure — Who played golf on the moon?

 Science & Tech — What fastening was inspired by observations of burdock seeds clinging to clothes?

 True or False? — Sex was the 'original sin' that had Adam and Eve expelled from the Garden of Eden; true or false?

ANSWERS: PAGE 181

Food & Drink
What useful digestive function do the leaves and pods of the senna plant perform?

Natural World
Which northern Scottish island gave its name to a style of pullover?

History
What were the three estates traditionally seen as making up the medieval kingdom?

Culture & Belief
The Royal Company of Archers serve as the Queen's bodyguard in which country?

Stage & Screen
Which actor appeared as Ivanhoe, The Saint and James Bond?

Written Word
After Bonkers the dog bit Garp's ear, how did Garp get his own back?

Music
Deacon Blue took their name from a track by which band?

Famous People
Derek Hatton was a councillor in which English city?

Sport & Leisure
Royal Blackheath is the oldest what in England?

Science & Tech
Which two architectural orders are combined in the composite order?

True or False?
The term 'Art Deco' came into use in the mid 1920s; true or false?

ANSWERS: PAGE 182

Food & Drink — What is sodium chloride more commonly known as?

Natural World — What small aquatic creature has the Latin name *hippocampus*?

History — The name of an art movement, what does the word 'dada' mean?

Culture & Belief — Helvetia is the Latin name for what country?

Stage & Screen — Where did the first cinema in the UK open?

Written Word — What Greek letter has come to mean a very small amount?

Music — Which musical impresario had hits as Bubblerock, Sakkarin, Shag and 100 Ton and a Feather?

Famous People — Who was the last English monarch to remain unmarried throughout their reign?

Sport & Leisure — Who played in the longest ever Wimbledon match?

Science & Tech — Where in a classroom might you see Mercator's Projection?

True or False? — The zodiac sign of Aquarius has the amethyst as its birth stone; true or false?

ANSWERS: PAGE 182

Food & Drink

What is the difference between oil and fat?

 Natural World

What river flows into the sea at New York?

 History

Who wrote the imperialist poem *The White Man's Burden* in 1899?

 Culture & Belief

Which Irish town gaves its name to a five-line poem?

 Stage & Screen

In what year did the number of colour films released in Britain first exceed the black and white ones?

 Written Word

The film *Schindler's List* was based on which book by Thomas Keneally?

 Music

What '70s band included guitarists Overend Watts and Ariel Bender?

 Famous People

In what year did Louis Bleriot become the first person to fly across the English Channel?

 Sport & Leisure

In what sport would you perform a christie?

 Science & Tech

Which company sold the first instant coffee?

 True or False?

The maximum number of times a piece of paper can be folded in half is seven; true or false?

ANSWERS: PAGE 183

Food & Drink

What type of tree is the source of sago?

Natural World

Peruvian guano was first used as a fertilizer in the 1840s. What is guano?

History

What century saw the end of the Chinese Ming dynasty?

Culture & Belief

In Scandinavian mythology whose souls went to Valhalla?

Stage & Screen

What film did Charlie Chaplin first speak in?

Written Word

What is the subject of Horace McCoy's *They Shoot Horses, Don't They*?

Music

Who was the bald-headed singer in Classix Nouveau?

Famous People

Alfred the Great founded which one of the three modern-day armed services?

Sport & Leisure

Which sport is played for the Davis Cup?

Science & Tech

What was made by the Manhattan Project?

True or False?

A dowry was originally brought to a marriage by the male partner; true or false?

ANSWERS: PAGE 183

Food & Drink
Which bottled water used the advertising slogan 'L'eau and behold'?

Natural World
What Scottish county is Gretna Green in?

History
Which sultanate and empire was known in the 19th and early 20th centuries as the 'sick man of Europe'?

Culture & Belief
Terence Rattigan dedicated *The Winslow Boy* to which boy who later became one of Mrs Thatcher's cabinet?

Stage & Screen
When did Superman first appear on TV (to within two years)?

Written Word
In which year was Orwell's *1984* published?

Music
Hamlet Cigars' adverts have become identified with which piece of music by J. S. Bach?

Famous People
Name the city where David Dinkins was the first black mayor.

Sport & Leisure
Which English football team dropped Woolwich from its name?

Science & Tech
The first paper hankies, Celluwipes, were given which new name by manufacturers Kimberley-Clark?

True or False?
Shredded Wheat was the first commercially produced breakfast cereal; true or false?

ANSWERS: PAGE 184

Which drinks company sponsors the comedy award at the Edinburgh Festival Fringe?

 Of stalactites and stalagmites, which grows upwards?

 What term was given to the ritual of prostrating oneself before the Chinese emperor?

 Which low, stuffed seat with no back is named after the Turkish empire?

 Which Hollywood superstar established the Sundance Institute to promote independent movie-making?

 Who wrote *Jaws*?

 Who was the long-tongued star of Bad Manners?

 Golfer Vijay Singh is a native of which country?

 Who was the last amateur to win the Open golf championship?

 What was the first ready-to-eat breakfast cereal?

 A Batmitzvah is the female equivalent of a Barmitzvah; true or false?

ANSWERS: PAGE 184

Food & Drink
Rickets is caused by a deficiency of which vitamin?

Natural World
Phobos and Deimos are moons of which planet?

History
George Bernard Shaw and H. G. Wells were members of which socialist group?

Culture & Belief
Which country was Mikhail Baryshnikov in when he defected to the west?

Stage & Screen
Jack Lemmon was one half of *The Odd Couple*; who was the other half?

Written Word
How many husbands had Scarlett O'Hara before Rhett Butler?

Music
Which 1980s band took their name from a tin of paint?

Famous People
What was Oscar Wilde's second given name?

Sport & Leisure
How many times did Sir Gordon Richards win the Derby?

Science & Tech
What type of wind is represented by 12 on the Beaufort scale?

True or False?
Boxer Joe Frazier was known as 'the Brown Bomber'; true or false?

ANSWERS: PAGE 185

Food & Drink
How do green vegetables differ from root vegetables?

Natural World
Which animal is a cross between a male ass and a female horse?

History
Who was the 'Sea-Green Incorruptible' who led the reign of terror in revoluntionary France?

Culture & Belief
What was the difference between a highwayman and a footpad?

Stage & Screen
Which canine star left her prints on the cement outside Mann's Chinese Theater?

Written Word
Which writer of fantasy wrote *The Earthsea Trilogy*?

Music
Who played Che Guevara in the original London cast of *Evita*?

Famous People
Whose gang were the perpetrators of the St Valentine's Day Massacre?

Sport & Leisure
In the 1970s, which horse racing trophy did Sagaro win three times?

Science & Tech
Which institutions benefit from using the Dewey decimal system?

True or False?
The original Greek Olympic Games took place every 10 years; true or false?

ANSWERS: PAGE 185

Food & Drink

Name one of TV's *Two Fat Ladies*.

Natural World

What is the main town of Jersey?

History

The Chrysler Airflow was a commercially unsuccessful but very influential design of what?

Culture & Belief

Ravi Shankar was an exponent of which musical instrument?

Stage & Screen

Who was the longest-serving Dr Who?

Written Word

What was W. Somerset Maugham's first name?

Music

What number overture was ELO's first hit?

Famous People

Which famous widow did Aristotle Onassis marry in 1968?

Sport & Leisure

Who, in 1977, was the first snooker player to win the World Championship with a two-piece cue?

Science & Tech

Which professional people might be fellows of the RIBA?

True or False?

A baby whale is called a foal; true or false?

ANSWERS: PAGE 186

Food & Drink
Which has more calories, a pint of lager, a pint of cider or a can of coke?

Natural World
How would a python kill its prey?

History
In an essay in 1734, what did Alexander Pope say is the proper study of mankind?

Culture & Belief
Waitangi Day is a national holiday in which country?

Stage & Screen
What 1942 classic is the most frequently shown film on US TV?

Written Word
Who is the professor who narrates Nabokov's *Lolita*?

Music
Which singer/songwriter sang 'I'll have to say I love you in a song'?

Famous People
Who was the first US president who was neither elected president nor vice-president?

Sport & Leisure
What was Ray Reardon's occupation before he became a snooker professional?

Science & Tech
What was the trademark name for the plastic resin developed by Leo Baekeland?

True or False?
A 50p piece has seven edges; true or false?

ANSWERS: PAGE 186

Food & Drink
Which cooking ingredient was developed from the Paisley textile trade?

Natural World
At what age do human males reach half their adult height?

History
Which car manufacturer made the Anglia?

Culture & Belief
How were the great plagues of the Middle Ages transmitted?

Stage & Screen
Who or what was 'Alex' in the title of the film, *Ice Cold In Alex*?

Written Word
Who wrote *Cat on a Hot Tin Roof*?

Music
What was the Troggs' only number 1?

Famous People
What title was held by Irish soldier and statesman Arthur Wellesley?

Sport & Leisure
Which racecourse hosts the Scottish Grand National?

Science & Tech
The first example of what device was fitted by Blaupunkt into a Studebaker?

True or False?
The first car speedometers only went up to 35 mph; true or false?

ANSWERS: PAGE 187

Food & Drink

What would you buy from a bodega?

 Natural World

What kind of creature is a flying fox?

 History

What was the first successful English colony, commemorating Elizabeth I in its name?

 Culture & Belief

What do we call the day before All Saints' Day?

 Stage & Screen

Which actor, famous for playing Dracula, was born in Transylvania?

 Written Word

Who wrote short stories called *A Perfect Day for Bananafish* and *For Esme, With Love and Squalor*?

 Music

Who released a single in the shape of the African continent?

 Famous People

How is Karol Wojtyla better known?

 Sport & Leisure

Which racecourse is the home of the Kentucky Derby?

 Science & Tech

What was a Stutz Bearcat?

 True or False?

Model-T Fords were always black; true or false?

ANSWERS: PAGE 187

Food & Drink
What nut gives flavour to ratafia?

Natural World
What is a young hare called?

History
When was the Berlin Wall pulled down?

Culture & Belief
Which symbol untied the followers of York and Lancaster?

Stage & Screen
Who was Emma Peel's replacement in the original *Avengers* TV series?

Written Word
What does Holden Caulfied say he will be, in the title of a book by J. D. Salinger?

Music
What, ironically, was the Rolling Stones' first number 1 hit?

Famous People
Who was the second man to walk on the moon?

Sport & Leisure
What major race is run at Longchamp?

Science & Tech
Which speech from Shakespeare was recited on the first public demonstration of the telephone?

True or False?
There are 13 red and white stripes on the American flag; true or false?

ANSWERS: PAGE 188

Food & Drink — Which name, from an Italian city, is given to a two- or three-flavoured ice cream?

 Natural World — Which island group includes Mallorca, Menorca and Ibiza?

 History — Early digital watches featured LED displays. What does LED stand for?

 Culture & Belief — Which Greek philosopher was taught by Socrates, and in turn taught Aristotle?

 Stage & Screen — What cinematic award was originally nicknamed a Stella?

 Written Word — How many lines are in a sonnet?

 Music — Which opera features the *Toreador's Song*?

 Famous People — Which entertainer insured his distinctive front teeth for £4million?

 Sport & Leisure — At what distance was Roger Black British number one?

 Science & Tech — Bell made the first long-distance telephone call in 1892 between which two American cities?

 True or False? — Jim Clark was the first to win the world motor racing driver's championship posthumously; true or false?

ANSWERS: PAGE 188

Food & Drink — Which food manufacturer sponsors Norwich City FC?

Natural World — Which stretch of water separates the Isle of Wight from the mainland?

History — How far, to the nearest 10 metres, could a skilled medieval longbowman fire a deadly arrow?

Culture & Belief — Who brought news to illiterate townspeople in past centuries?

Stage & Screen — What does BAFTA stand for?

Written Word — Which writer's first names are John Ronald Reuel?

Music — What instruction was the title of Cliff Richard's first hit?

Famous People — Where is Karl Marx buried?

Sport & Leisure — Hakkinen and Coulthard drove for which Formula 1 team in 1998?

Science & Tech — If contours connect points of equal height on a map, what do isobaths connect?

True or False? — The French spirit Calvados is made from fermented apples; true or false?

ANSWERS: PAGE 189

Food & Drink

Fray Bentos is a port in which country?

Natural World

Niagara Falls is between which two Great Lakes?

History

How many pennies were in an old style British pound?

Culture & Belief

On a map of the London Underground, which line is coloured grey?

Stage & Screen

What now regular event took place at Hollywood's Roosevelt Hotel on 16 May 1929?

Written Word

According to Jeanette Winterson, what are oranges not?

Music

Johnny Wakelin had two hits with songs about which sportsman?

Famous People

What was Nazi wartime propagandist William Joyce better known as?

Sport & Leisure

Which British sporting venue includes the Paddock Hill grandstand?

Science & Tech

What was the innovative feature of the Rolex 'Oyster' watch?

True or False?

By law, Scotch whisky must be left for five years after distilling before it can be sold; true or false?

ANSWERS: PAGE 189

Food & Drink
TVP is made from soya, but what does TVP stand for?

Natural World
What are the names of the two falls that make up Niagara?

History
Which company did a yellow bird called Busby advertise?

Culture & Belief
Which coin bears the phrase 'Standing on the shoulders of giants'?

Stage & Screen
How many members does the Academy of Motion Picture Arts and Sciences have (to the nearest 100)?

Written Word
In the books by P. G. Wodehouse, whose manservant is Jeeves?

Music
In the Elvis song, what was the name of his latest flame?

Famous People
What famous hotel is named after the founder of Singapore?

Sport & Leisure
Which card game features his heels and his nobs?

Science & Tech
What term was coined in 1937 to describe a stock of human blood for transfusions?

True or False?
Rembrandt painted *The Laughing Cavalier*; true or false?

ANSWERS: PAGE 190

Food & Drink

What ingredient forms the topping on crème brûlée?

Natural World

Which Scottish island group features Skara Brae, Scapa Flow and the Old Man of Hoy?

History

Whose first volume of war memoirs was called *Adolf Hitler: My Part in his Downfall*?

Culture & Belief

In pantomine, whose sweetheart was Columbine?

Stage & Screen

How tall, to the nearest inch, is an Oscar statuette?

Written Word

Who is the salesman in Arthur Miller's *Death of a Salesman*?

Music

Who wrote the Monkees' hit *I'm a Believer*?

Famous People

After the Vietnam war, what was the new name for Saigon?

Sport & Leisure

Donald and Malcolm Campbell both drove vehicles with which name?

Science & Tech

Which item of office stationery do the French call 'trombones'?

True or False?

The Smurfs were originally known as Les Schtroumpfs; true or false?

ANSWERS: PAGE 190

SECTION TWO

THE QUIZ BOOK *ANSWERS*

SETS 1 – 120

SET 1

Food & Drink	Drambuie
Natural World	Armenia
History	11
Culture & Belief	Honey bees
Stage & Screen	Tinky Winky
Written Word	The Thompson Twins
Music	There were three of them
Famous People	John Gummer
Sport & Leisure	Darts
Science & Tech	Meccano
True or False?	True

SET 2

Food & Drink	Russia
Natural World	Beer
History	England's medieval wealth from wool
Culture & Belief	The Lord Chancellor
Stage & Screen	Dipsy
Written Word	Tin Tin's
Music	Cherry pink and apple blossom white
Famous People	Carrots
Sport & Leisure	Brown
Science & Tech	Brown
True or False?	True

SET 3

Food & Drink	7lbs (3.2kg)
Natural World	Kent
History	Madrid
Culture & Belief	Madrid
Stage & Screen	*Due South*
Written Word	The cruellest month
Music	Fats
Famous People	Canterbury Cathedral
Sport & Leisure	Seven
Science & Tech	The earth
True or False?	False (it was Wilkie Collins)

SET 4

Food & Drink	Ten
Natural World	Both male and female
History	Buttons at the cuff
Culture & Belief	St Paul's
Stage & Screen	$250,000
Written Word	Sherlock Holmes
Music	Maurice (by one hour)
Famous People	The Nation of Islam
Sport & Leisure	Elephant
Science & Tech	Red, yellow, blue
True or False?	False

SET 5

Food & Drink	Mad cow disease
Natural World	Central Park
History	Minister of Propaganda
Culture & Belief	Right
Stage & Screen	Homer, Marge, Bart, Lisa, Maggie

Written Word	One day it'll keep you
Music	*Whole Lotta Love*
Famous People	Charles Stewart Parnell; Oscar Wilde
Sport & Leisure	5 feet
Science & Tech	Three (red, green, blue)
True or False?	False (red, yellow and blue)

SET 6

Food & Drink	Soya-bean curd
Natural World	New York (Central Park)
History	Lady Godiva
Culture & Belief	A book
Stage & Screen	Smithers

Written Word	Albert Einstein
Music	Led Zeppelin
Famous People	11th
Sport & Leisure	Tug-of-war
Science & Tech	Cast iron
True or False?	False

SET 7

Food & Drink	Mushrooms
Natural World	20 sq ft
History	Two
Culture & Belief	Faith, hope and charity
Stage & Screen	Jane Russell

Written Word	Brunettes
Music	James
Famous People	36
Sport & Leisure	One
Science & Tech	Dolly (the sheep)
True or False?	False (it was the Tornados' Telstar)

SET 8

Food & Drink	Stuff a mushroom
Natural World	12
History	Catherine
Culture & Belief	East of Eden
Stage & Screen	Jaclyn Smith, Kate Jackson, Farrah Fawcett (-Majors)

Written Word	Cain
Music	*Lucy in the Sky with Diamonds*
Famous People	George Harrison
Sport & Leisure	London
Science & Tech	Pi (π)
True or False?	True

SET 9

Food & Drink	Dried insects
Natural World	The mosquito
History	Two
Culture & Belief	12
Stage & Screen	The Goons
Written Word	Beelzebub
Music	The Rolling Stones
Famous People	Francis Chichester
Sport & Leisure	He ran the race barefoot
Science & Tech	3.14 or $^{22}/_7$
True or False?	True

SET 10

Food & Drink	4
Natural World	X
History	Brother-in-law
Culture & Belief	Thor
Stage & Screen	Anakin Skywalker
Written Word	*Blade Runner*
Music	Frank Sinatra
Famous People	Bing Crosby
Sport & Leisure	Zola Budd
Science & Tech	Celsius
True or False?	True

SET 11

| Written Word | Hamlet |

| Food & Drink | Bromine |

| Music | Siobhan Fahey was a member of both |

| Natural World | 23 |

| Famous People | Frank Sinatra |

| History | A wall-hanging |

| Sport & Leisure | Uruguay |

| Culture & Belief | Transport & General Workers' Union |

| Science & Tech | Belfast |

| Stage & Screen | Borsetshire |

| True or False? | False (it is Falstaff) |

SET 12

| Written Word | A hedgehog |

| Food & Drink | Trifle |

| Music | The paintings on your wall |

| Natural World | Tunisia |

| Famous People | Orson Welles |

| History | It was awarded to Malta in 1942 |

| Sport & Leisure | The Marathon |

| Culture & Belief | The George Cross |

| Science & Tech | Blackpool |

| Stage & Screen | Harry Lime |

| True or False? | True |

SET 13

Food & Drink	Soup
Natural World	The iris
History	24
Culture & Belief	Good of themselves
Stage & Screen	*The Third Man*

Written Word	A troll
Music	A wooden chair
Famous People	William Randolph Hearst
Sport & Leisure	One
Science & Tech	365 ft
True or False?	False

SET 14

Food & Drink	Mayonnaise
Natural World	Lion and tiger
History	10
Culture & Belief	Love
Stage & Screen	Honor Blackman

Written Word	Christopher Robin
Music	Eternal
Famous People	Andy Warhol
Sport & Leisure	Rangers
Science & Tech	The Pyramids of Egypt
True or False?	True

SET 15

Food & Drink	Water
Natural World	120 in (300 cm)
History	4
Culture & Belief	Cancer, Scorpio and Pisces
Stage & Screen	Mrs Goggins
Written Word	*The Water Margin*
Music	7 swans a-swimming
Famous People	William Wordsworth
Sport & Leisure	Synchronised swimming
Science & Tech	Water
True or False?	True

SET 16

Food & Drink	Flaky
Natural World	Chicago
History	William the Conqueror
Culture & Belief	A secret never to be told
Stage & Screen	Steve Coogan
Written Word	Robert Burns
Music	*Viva España*
Famous People	Two
Sport & Leisure	Manchester
Science & Tech	Greenwich Observatory
True or False?	False

SET 17

Food & Drink	Thousand leaves
Natural World	12,000 miles
History	600 BC
Culture & Belief	Lancelot
Stage & Screen	Sam Peckinpah
Written Word	The cheque book
Music	Anni-Frid (Frida)
Famous People	He was an MP
Sport & Leisure	Cards
Science & Tech	The Humber
True or False?	True

SET 18

Food & Drink	Stilton
Natural World	Avebury
History	The Hole in the Wall Gang
Culture & Belief	The Angel of the North
Stage & Screen	Butch Cassidy and the Sundance Kid
Written Word	He was already married
Music	The Marseillaise
Famous People	Maria Callas
Sport & Leisure	Marco Pantani
Science & Tech	The Michelin Man
True or False?	False

SET 19

Food & Drink	Bacteria
Natural World	The Dominican Republic & Haiti
History	Haiti
Culture & Belief	The first harvest of the first settlers
Stage & Screen	Perdita or Pongo
Written Word	George Bernard Shaw wrote it
Music	Van Morrison
Famous People	Noël Coward
Sport & Leisure	British Open, US Open, US Masters, US PGA
Science & Tech	Different colours
True or False?	False

SET 20

Food & Drink	Preserved beef on rye bread
Natural World	The moon
History	USSR
Culture & Belief	Capricorn
Stage & Screen	Pluto
Written Word	Big Brother
Music	*That's Amore*
Famous People	Gene Roddenberry and Timothy Leary
Sport & Leisure	Three
Science & Tech	Nine
True or False?	False (she appeared in the original series)

SET 21

Food & Drink	Green
Natural World	The Shetland Islands
History	The NHS
Culture & Belief	The crucifixion of Christ
Stage & Screen	Ron Moody
Written Word	Leslie Halliwell
Music	Mike McGear
Famous People	Michael Fagin
Sport & Leisure	Canada
Science & Tech	Harris tweed
True or False?	False (it is the Falabella)

SET 22

Food & Drink	Bicarbonate of soda
Natural World	32
History	It brought the first West Indian immigrants
Culture & Belief	Easter
Stage & Screen	Toothpaste
Written Word	Long John Silver
Music	The Scaffold
Famous People	Samoa
Sport & Leisure	1968
Science & Tech	60 degrees
True or False?	True

SET 23

Food & Drink	Ministry of Agriculture, Fisheries & Food
Natural World	The USA
History	1776
Culture & Belief	Go to sleep (it's a sleeping pill)
Stage & Screen	Kojak
Written Word	He had a lean and hungry look
Music	Ginger Baker, Jack Bruce, Eric Clapton
Famous People	Twiggy
Sport & Leisure	8 stones
Science & Tech	Four
True or False?	False

SET 24

Food & Drink	Tea
Natural World	Vermont
History	America won independence in 1776
Culture & Belief	Samaritan
Stage & Screen	*The Likely Lads* and *Whatever Happened to the Likely Lads?*
Written Word	Captain Flint
Music	*Tubular Bells* by Mike Oldfield
Famous People	America (the continent)
Sport & Leisure	Every three years
Science & Tech	UK (in 1936, three years before the USA)
True or False?	True

SET 25

Food & Drink	Pineapple
Natural World	Breastbone
History	George Washington
Culture & Belief	Killing the hydra
Stage & Screen	Gerald Scarfe

Written Word	House-For-One
Music	Ray and Dave Davies
Famous People	Gerald Scarfe
Sport & Leisure	Joe Davis
Science & Tech	Collar bone
True or False?	False

SET 26

Food & Drink	Both are soups, served cold
Natural World	Paradoxical or REM
History	Carnaby Street
Culture & Belief	13
Stage & Screen	Clint Eastwood

Written Word	Anthony Burgess
Music	*Cockles & Mussels, Alive, Alive-O*
Famous People	Jeremy Irons
Sport & Leisure	Brazil
Science & Tech	She was the first woman in space
True or False?	True

SET 27

Food & Drink — Red wine

Natural World — Rapid Eye Movement

History — He was the first PM to be assassinated

Culture & Belief — Walk along it (it's a country lane)

Stage & Screen — Fr Jack

Written Word — Left (*My Left Foot*)

Music — The Labour Party

Famous People — Robin Cook

Sport & Leisure — 7

Science & Tech — 28

True or False? — False

SET 28

Food & Drink — Brandy

Natural World — They carry and suckle their young in body pouches

History — Pompeii

Culture & Belief — Pub signs (outdoor)

Stage & Screen — *The X-Files*

Written Word — Mr Sparks

Music — Andrew Ridgeley

Famous People — Journalist

Sport & Leisure — Scotland

Science & Tech — 14

True or False? — False (it is 'Q')

SET 29

Food & Drink	Roughage
Natural World	An albatross
History	Cigarette advertising
Culture & Belief	No
Stage & Screen	Ross and Monica

Written Word	He is a taxi-driver
Music	It was their 1st non-Beatles US no 1
Famous People	The Beatles
Sport & Leisure	A raised deck at a ship's rear
Science & Tech	Liver
True or False?	False (it's women's fragrances)

SET 30

Food & Drink	None
Natural World	Yellow
History	She was the first woman elected MP
Culture & Belief	Beautiful women
Stage & Screen	Bond girls

Written Word	Dr No
Music	Men at Work
Famous People	Bob Holness
Sport & Leisure	A catamaran
Science & Tech	Gold
True or False?	True

SET 31

Food & Drink	C
Natural World	4500
History	Before the American Civil War
Culture & Belief	Nicene, Apostles and Athanasian
Stage & Screen	*Listen With Mother*

Written Word	A Babylonian King
Music	Jimmy Young
Famous People	John Adams
Sport & Leisure	On *Gladiators* TV show
Science & Tech	1kg
True or False?	True

SET 32

Food & Drink	Fat
Natural World	Oxford
History	The Nazi Party
Culture & Belief	Diana
Stage & Screen	Pluto

Written Word	1931
Music	The Sex Pistols
Famous People	Walt Disney
Sport & Leisure	Hammersmith and Barnes
Science & Tech	1868
True or False?	True

SET 33

Food & Drink	Yeast extract	Written Word	Jack Kerouac
Natural World	A troop	Music	A coolabah tree
History	Knight of the Thistle	Famous People	Steven Spielberg
Culture & Belief	Paddle in it	Sport & Leisure	Goolagong
Stage & Screen	The name shows the film's director disowned it	Science & Tech	Amsterdam
		True or False?	True

SET 34

Food & Drink	Atlanta, Georgia	Written Word	All the perfumes of Arabia
Natural World	The Canaries	Music	Waylon Jennings
History	Macbeth	Famous People	Pope
Culture & Belief	East Timor	Sport & Leisure	Foil
Stage & Screen	A Volkswagen Beetle	Science & Tech	Jupiter
		True or False?	True

SET 35

| Written Word | Open sesame |

| Food & Drink | Dyspepsia (indigestion) |

| Music | John Lennon |

| Natural World | Indigestion |

| Famous People | Warren Beatty (her brother) |

| History | Nelson |

| Sport & Leisure | He is left-handed |

| Culture & Belief | I think, therefore I am |

| Science & Tech | 18 |

| Stage & Screen | Alan Ladd (in *Shane*) |

| True or False? | False (it is Mandarin) |

SET 36

| Written Word | Ali Baba |

| Food & Drink | Homepride |

| Music | *You Never Can Tell* |

| Natural World | Crocus |

| Famous People | Sharon Stone |

| History | The Gregorian calendar |

| Sport & Leisure | Bobby Jones |

| Culture & Belief | August |

| Science & Tech | 180° |

| Stage & Screen | *The Pit and the Pendulum* |

| True or False? | True (it lasted 115 years) |

SET 37

Food & Drink	Honey
Natural World	15
History	Edward II
Culture & Belief	Christmas
Stage & Screen	Callahan

Written Word	Isaac Asimov
Music	Flodden
Famous People	Buddhism
Sport & Leisure	0-0
Science & Tech	Halley's Comet
True or False?	False (it would be quick and lively)

SET 38

Food & Drink	20
Natural World	K-2
History	Wat Tyler
Culture & Belief	Abraham
Stage & Screen	They all subsequently became sitcoms

Written Word	Emily
Music	Tchaikovsky
Famous People	Richard Gere and Cindy Crawford
Sport & Leisure	It's higher in the centre
Science & Tech	75 years
True or False?	False

SET 39

Food & Drink	Basil
Natural World	The Tropic of Cancer ($23\frac{1}{2}°$N)
History	Richard II
Culture & Belief	Virgo
Stage & Screen	FAB 1

Written Word	Melvyn Bragg
Music	*Pathetique*
Famous People	Bill Gates
Sport & Leisure	An angler (these are knots)
Science & Tech	Disk operating system
True or False?	False (it was Ararat)

SET 40

Food & Drink	Wheat flour
Natural World	A fish
History	Jack the Ripper
Culture & Belief	Death
Stage & Screen	Frank Oz (he operated both)

Written Word	In a horse-riding accident
Music	Marc Bolan and Bing Crosby
Famous People	He played himself
Sport & Leisure	Muhammad Ali
Science & Tech	Star Wars
True or False?	False (it was England)

SET 41

Food & Drink	Fruits or seeds
Natural World	Captain Cook
History	Korea
Culture & Belief	The Magic Circle
Stage & Screen	The Banana Splits

Written Word	Julian Barnes
Music	Spiceworld – The Movie
Famous People	Nelson Mandela and F. W. de Klerk
Sport & Leisure	England and Australia
Science & Tech	Three hours
True or False?	False

SET 42

Food & Drink	Cereal (Ceres)
Natural World	The Sandwich Isles
History	Roy Jenkins and William Rodgers
Culture & Belief	Apollo
Stage & Screen	Groundhog Day

Written Word	Molesworth
Music	KC and the Sunshine Band
Famous People	Damien Hirst
Sport & Leisure	The museum at Lord's
Science & Tech	Gabriel Fahrenheit
True or False?	True

SET 43

Food & Drink	Salt
Natural World	Alaska
History	The Suffragettes
Culture & Belief	*Zeitgeist*
Stage & Screen	Baldrick

Written Word	24
Music	Dora Bryan
Famous People	Lady Jane Grey: 'The Nine-day Queen'
Sport & Leisure	Franz Beckenbauer
Science & Tech	Panama Canal
True or False?	True

SET 44

Food & Drink	A bat
Natural World	Dover, Hastings, Hythe, Romney and Sandwich
History	Emmeline Pankhurst
Culture & Belief	The emperor of Japan
Stage & Screen	The *Carry On* films

Written Word	Thomas the Tank Engine
Music	Gilbert and Sullivan
Famous People	Ceylon
Sport & Leisure	Surfing
Science & Tech	The Mercedes Benz car
True or False?	False

SET 45

Food & Drink	Pasteurisation
Natural World	Pancreas
History	Corazon Aquino
Culture & Belief	On a baby's bottom
Stage & Screen	The *Carry On* films

Written Word	Sodor
Music	Neil Innes
Famous People	Literature
Sport & Leisure	Croquet
Science & Tech	Pierre and Marie Curie
True or False?	True

SET 46

Food & Drink	A dried plum
Natural World	Pearl Harbour
History	The Brownie
Culture & Belief	Your car would have had a minor shunt
Stage & Screen	*Carry on ... Up The Khyber*

Written Word	Charlie Chaplin
Music	*A Hard Day's Night*
Famous People	Jimmy Saville
Sport & Leisure	Surfing
Science & Tech	Sony and Philips
True or False?	False (Key West, Florida)

SET 47

Food & Drink	Tate & Lyle
Natural World	Bile
History	Britain
Culture & Belief	Sad
Stage & Screen	*Due South*
Written Word	*The Taming Of The Shrew*
Music	Suzi Quatro
Famous People	Frank Sinatra
Sport & Leisure	John Curry
Science & Tech	Tate and Lyle
True or False?	False

SET 48

Food & Drink	Grapefruit and tangerine
Natural World	The Caribbean
History	Elizabeth I
Culture & Belief	A leap
Stage & Screen	Robert De Niro
Written Word	*To Kill a Mockingbird*
Music	*Deliverance*
Famous People	Elizabeth Barrett & Robert Browning
Sport & Leisure	Mexico
Science & Tech	Electric and Musical Industries
True or False?	True

SET 49

Written Word		*West Side Story*	
Food & Drink	Sour cabbage	**Music**	Willy Russell
Natural World	The blue whale	**Famous People**	Anne Boleyn
History	Queen Anne	**Sport & Leisure**	Mary, Queen of Scots
Culture & Belief	Matthew	**Science & Tech**	Smallpox
Stage & Screen	*Frasier*	**True or False?**	True

SET 50

Written Word		Vito Corleone	
Food & Drink	Pregnant women	**Music**	*Head*
Natural World	California	**Famous People**	The US Army Air Force
History	The Arts and Crafts Movement	**Sport & Leisure**	Nadia Comaneci
Culture & Belief	S4C (Welsh language TV service)	**Science & Tech**	Obstetrician
Stage & Screen	Crane	**True or False?**	False (it is the Czechs)

SET 51

Food & Drink
Mashed turnip

Natural World
The Spey

History
Hong Kong

Culture & Belief
The War Cry

Stage & Screen
Bonanza

Written Word
Major Major Major Major

Music
Miss Saigon

Famous People
Mick Jagger

Sport & Leisure
Diamond

Science & Tech
Diamond

True or False?
False

SET 52

Food & Drink
19

Natural World
Lindisfarne

History
Seaplanes

Culture & Belief
In a grandstand

Stage & Screen
Dr Who

Written Word
An engineering company

Music
You'll Never Walk Alone

Famous People
Iona

Sport & Leisure
Nine

Science & Tech
Glasgow Central and London Euston

True or False?
True

SET 53

Food & Drink	Ultra heat-treated	**Written Word**	Utopia
Natural World	The liver	**Music**	*Shake, Rattle and Roll*
History	1936	**Famous People**	William Bligh
Culture & Belief	He helped carry his cross to Calvary	**Sport & Leisure**	Diego Maradonna
Stage & Screen	Three	**Science & Tech**	1
		True or False?	True

SET 54

Food & Drink	Rennet	**Written Word**	Kurt Vonnegut Jr.
Natural World	Through their skin	**Music**	*Blackboard Jungle*
History	Grandson	**Famous People**	Genghis Khan
Culture & Belief	The Apocrypha	**Sport & Leisure**	Both teams sank
Stage & Screen	*Blue Peter*	**Science & Tech**	Kitty Hawk
		True or False?	False (it was his brother Orville)

SET 55

| Written Word | Braemar |

| Food & Drink | Stale |

| Music | Val Kilmer |

| Natural World | Close their eyes |

| Famous People | Trafalgar |

| History | 1945 |

| Sport & Leisure | He was the first footballer to be knighted |

| Culture & Belief | Flying Squad (Sweeney Todd) |

| Science & Tech | *The Spirit of St Louis* |

| Stage & Screen | *Moonlighting* |

| True or False? | True |

SET 56

| Written Word | Don Quixote's horse |

| Food & Drink | Barley |

| Music | Xylophone |

| Natural World | Greenland |

| Famous People | Lewis Carroll |

| History | Franklin D. Roosevelt (1939) |

| Sport & Leisure | Lester Piggot |

| Culture & Belief | Shrove Tuesday, or Pancake Tuesday |

| Science & Tech | Aspirin |

| Stage & Screen | *The Man from UNCLE* |

| True or False? | False (it's 10) |

SET 57

Food & Drink	Bouquet garni
Natural World	Greenland
History	HMS Resolution
Culture & Belief	November
Stage & Screen	David McCallum

Written Word	John Updike
Music	Tubular Bells by Mike Oldfield
Famous People	Mathematics
Sport & Leisure	1993
Science & Tech	The biggest bicycle ever (73 ft long)
True or False?	False (it's Greenland)

SET 58

Food & Drink	Polenta
Natural World	Monaco
History	1970s
Culture & Belief	November
Stage & Screen	An Oscar statuette

Written Word	A white rabbit
Music	Denny Laine
Famous People	Ryan and Tatum O'Neal
Sport & Leisure	Red and green
Science & Tech	U
True or False?	False (it is Lenin)

SET 59

Food & Drink	Apple
Natural World	Nevada
History	1941
Culture & Belief	Mona Lisa
Stage & Screen	None
Written Word	*The English Patient*
Music	Little
Famous People	George C. Scott
Sport & Leisure	Croquet lawn
Science & Tech	*Tron*
True or False?	True

SET 60

Food & Drink	Garibaldi
Natural World	Staffa
History	Massachusetts
Culture & Belief	Hallowe'en
Stage & Screen	Saxophone
Written Word	*Midnight's Children*
Music	The Tommy Dorsey Band
Famous People	Fred Astaire
Sport & Leisure	Sporting Lisbon and Sunderland
Science & Tech	Aluminium
True or False?	True

SET 61

Food & Drink	Melba
Natural World	Purple
History	Caernarvon Castle
Culture & Belief	Fire
Stage & Screen	*Cabaret*

Written Word	*Waiting for Godot*
Music	Alexander O'Neal
Famous People	Find Dr Livingstone
Sport & Leisure	*Escape to Victory*
Science & Tech	RADAR
True or False?	True

SET 62

Food & Drink	Pears
Natural World	The Mid Ocean Ridge (in the Atlantic)
History	42
Culture & Belief	Remembrance
Stage & Screen	Dame Judi Dench

Written Word	Sitwell
Music	Jupiter
Famous People	Harry S. Truman
Sport & Leisure	The America's Cup
Science & Tech	Earth
True or False?	False

SET 63

Food & Drink	Grilling
Natural World	Russian Federation
History	22
Culture & Belief	1p
Stage & Screen	*Grease*

Written Word	*The Young Visiters*
Music	The Rezillos
Famous People	Ireland
Sport & Leisure	London, Paris or Los Angeles
Science & Tech	A nanosecond
True or False?	True

SET 64

Food & Drink	Peach
Natural World	Breadfruit
History	1086
Culture & Belief	Thou shalt have no other gods before me
Stage & Screen	Quasimodo

Written Word	*Treasure Island*
Music	The Stranglers (The Guildford Stranglers)
Famous People	The Kennedys
Sport & Leisure	42
Science & Tech	Uranus
True or False?	False (it's the fear of rain)

SET 65

Food & Drink
An alcoholic cocktail or an apple

Natural World
17th

History
Agincourt

Culture & Belief
78

Stage & Screen
The Oscar statuette

Written Word
Agincourt

Music
Jim Steinman

Famous People
Confederates

Sport & Leisure
8 points

Science & Tech
Hydrogen

True or False?
False (he is not on any)

SET 66

Food & Drink
Yes, cream cheese

Natural World
Istanbul

History
Patrick, George and Andrew

Culture & Belief
16

Stage & Screen
Crete

Written Word
Samuel Beckett

Music
Irving Berlin

Famous People
Lenin

Sport & Leisure
Argentina

Science & Tech
Plastic

True or False?
True

SET 67

| | | Written Word | Sir John Betjeman |

| Food & Drink | Tomatoes | Music | Cello |

| Natural World | Rust | Famous People | Beheaded |

| History | George III | Sport & Leisure | Basketball |

| Culture & Belief | 1984 | Science & Tech | Tupperware |

| Stage & Screen | *Cats* | True or False? | False (it's on Bedloe's Island) |

SET 68

| | | Written Word | Hilaire Belloc |

| Food & Drink | Basting | Music | Hovis |

| Natural World | Tasmania | Famous People | B&Q |

| History | Bikini | Sport & Leisure | Chicago Bulls |

| Culture & Belief | Jehovah's Witnesses | Science & Tech | Flush toilet |

| Stage & Screen | Jesus and Judas | True or False? | True |

SET 69

Category	Answer
Food & Drink	Largest
Natural World	Barn owl
History	*Titanic*
Culture & Belief	Dance
Stage & Screen	The George Cross
Written Word	Sexton Blake
Music	Maybelline
Famous People	Great-great-grandson
Sport & Leisure	Rod Laver
Science & Tech	Venus and Mercury
True or False?	False

SET 70

Category	Answer
Food & Drink	Loaves of bread
Natural World	Wyoming
History	325
Culture & Belief	The meek
Stage & Screen	*The X-Files Movie*
Written Word	American
Music	Ringo Starr
Famous People	Cinema
Sport & Leisure	Mark Spitz
Science & Tech	Red, blue, green
True or False?	True

SET 71

Food & Drink
Easter, Christmas or Mothering Sunday

Natural World
Liffey and Taff

History
Coal

Culture & Belief
Let there be light

Stage & Screen
Coronation Street

Written Word
Iain Banks

Music
Charlie Brown

Famous People
Margaret Thatcher

Sport & Leisure
Ski-ing and rifle-shooting

Science & Tech
High fidelity

True or False?
True

SET 72

Food & Drink
108

Natural World
Indian summer

History
Sandinistas

Culture & Belief
16th (1517)

Stage & Screen
He was a horse

Written Word
A fox-hunter

Music
Martin Luther King

Famous People
Martin Luther King

Sport & Leisure
St Leger

Science & Tech
Horsepower

True or False?
False (it was Chicago)

SET 73

Food & Drink	60
Natural World	Anglesey
History	Clothing
Culture & Belief	'Property is theft'
Stage & Screen	*Saturday Night Live*

Written Word	Canada
Music	Bob Geldof
Famous People	Canada
Sport & Leisure	Juan Fangio
Science & Tech	In a brick wall
True or False?	False (it goes around the waist)

SET 74

Food & Drink	Peanuts
Natural World	Ohio, Oklahoma, Oregon
History	Mao Tse Tung
Culture & Belief	Four
Stage & Screen	*Blue Peter*

Written Word	*Daily Express*
Music	Bernard Cribbins
Famous People	Leonid Brezhnev
Sport & Leisure	Betty Stove
Science & Tech	Helicopter
True or False?	True

SET 75

Food & Drink	Tax levied on a barrel	Written Word	Booze
Natural World	St George's Channel	Music	Bernie Taupin
History	Reaganomics	Famous People	In an air crash
Culture & Belief	Athene	Sport & Leisure	American football
Stage & Screen	The TARDIS	Science & Tech	On a £1 coin
		True or False?	False (it is the USA)

SET 76

Food & Drink	Choux	Written Word	*Barfly*
Natural World	Yellow	Music	Paul Weller, Bruce Foxton, Rick Buckler
History	6	Famous People	Orson Welles
Culture & Belief	Quakers	Sport & Leisure	Brazilian
Stage & Screen	Singapore, Utopia, Zanzibar, Morocco, Rio, Bali, Hong Kong	Science & Tech	7
		True or False?	False (it is the sheep)

SET 77

Written Word	Chaps

Food & Drink	Fish

Music	Mike Reid

Natural World	Mackerel

Famous People	Hans Christian Andersen

History	Sri Lanka

Sport & Leisure	Evander Holyfield

Culture & Belief	Buddha

Science & Tech	3

Stage & Screen	A nickel (5 cents)

True or False?	False (it is keys)

SET 78

Written Word	J and X

Food & Drink	Yellow

Music	Tuba

Natural World	Green

Famous People	On a tightrope

History	BEA and BOAC

Sport & Leisure	Adidas

Culture & Belief	It no longer says 'new' pence

Science & Tech	Suspension

Stage & Screen	Alexandra Palace

True or False?	True

SET 79

Food & Drink	Peru and Bolivia
Natural World	Brazil and Argentina
History	Nicaragua
Culture & Belief	Epiphany
Stage & Screen	On the spotlight to direct the beam

Written Word	Enemies
Music	Humphrey Lyttelton
Famous People	Harry Houdini
Sport & Leisure	New Zealand
Science & Tech	Photocopier
True or False?	True

SET 80

Food & Drink	Hazelnuts
Natural World	The Thames (at Oxford)
History	1976
Culture & Belief	2000
Stage & Screen	*Crossroads*

Written Word	Philip Marlowe
Music	Wold
Famous People	Abraham Lincoln
Sport & Leisure	Hockenheim
Science & Tech	Ohm
True or False?	False (it was Klapka)

SET 81

		Written Word	William Burroughs
Food & Drink	Liver	Music	Diana Ross and Lionel Ritchie
Natural World	Lizard Point	Famous People	Le Corbusier
History	General Galtieri	Sport & Leisure	Show jumping
Culture & Belief	Le Corbusier	Science & Tech	2
Stage & Screen	Ramsay Street	True or False?	False (it was London)

SET 82

		Written Word	*Tales of the City*
Food & Drink	Acetic acid	Music	50
Natural World	Superior	Famous People	Aristotle
History	Indira Gandhi	Sport & Leisure	US PGA
Culture & Belief	Women	Science & Tech	16
Stage & Screen	*Casablanca*	True or False?	False (they have four)

SET 83

Food & Drink
Unrefined sugar

Natural World
Hawaii

History
They were not related

Culture & Belief
Fido

Stage & Screen
Oxford, Glasgow and Amsterdam

Written Word
Bob Dylan

Music
Poland

Famous People
Suicide

Sport & Leisure
Kevin Curran

Science & Tech
Hovercraft

True or False?
True

SET 84

Food & Drink
Tapioca

Natural World
Gemini

History
Almost 3 years (2 years 361 days)

Culture & Belief
Duplex

Stage & Screen
Dublin, Glasgow and Sheffield

Written Word
India gained its independence

Music
Number 8

Famous People
Tutankhamun's tomb

Sport & Leisure
Glorious

Science & Tech
The Flying Scotsman

True or False?
False (it was 12 seconds)

SET 85

Food & Drink	Scurvy
Natural World	The Alps
History	Bangladesh
Culture & Belief	On a cheque card
Stage & Screen	*Monty Python's Flying Circus*

Written Word	Loch Katrine
Music	Nat 'King' Cole
Famous People	Charles Darwin
Sport & Leisure	300
Science & Tech	Galvanised
True or False?	True

SET 86

Food & Drink	Wheat (semolina)
Natural World	From east to west
History	Jawaharlal Nehru
Culture & Belief	Thursday
Stage & Screen	Terry Gilliam

Written Word	Jimmy Durante
Music	*Release Me*
Famous People	Horatio Nelson
Sport & Leisure	Sandy Lyle
Science & Tech	The solar system
True or False?	False

SET 87

Food & Drink	Haggis
Natural World	Majorca
History	Lord Louis Mountbatten
Culture & Belief	£500
Stage & Screen	Felix (a cat; the others are dogs)
Written Word	Clive James
Music	Funky
Famous People	Henry VII
Sport & Leisure	India
Science & Tech	Distance
True or False?	False (it is St Andrew's)

SET 88

Food & Drink	Shells
Natural World	Southern
History	Indonesia
Culture & Belief	The Isle of Man's Tynwald
Stage & Screen	Daktari
Written Word	Private Eye (Richard Ingrams)
Music	Drums and flute
Famous People	Uranus
Sport & Leisure	Harold Dennis Bird
Science & Tech	Kew
True or False?	False (it was Kalinin)

SET 89

Food & Drink	One hour
Natural World	One
History	Spiro Agnew
Culture & Belief	Japan
Stage & Screen	Vietnam, the First World War and the Second World War

Written Word	E. J. Thribbs
Music	Seven
Famous People	Sir Edwin Landseer
Sport & Leisure	Don Bradman
Science & Tech	Singer
True or False?	True

SET 90

Food & Drink	Lancashire
Natural World	Aardvark
History	*Glasnost*
Culture & Belief	Cavaliers & Roundheads (Parliamentarians & Royalists)
Stage & Screen	Mickey Mouse

Written Word	Bill Bryson
Music	16
Famous People	Milan
Sport & Leisure	Ian Botham
Science & Tech	Calico
True or False?	True

SET 91

Written Word		Quotations	
Food & Drink	Houses of Parliament	Music	Elvis Presley
Natural World	Herring	Famous People	Richard Nixon
History	1961	Sport & Leisure	Surrey (7)
Culture & Belief	Rampant	Science & Tech	Shoes
Stage & Screen	Eli Wallach	True or False?	False (it was Ecuador)

SET 92

Written Word		Topsy (*Uncle Tom's Cabin*)	
Food & Drink	A slice of lemon	Music	Jerry Hall
Natural World	Spring	Famous People	1660s
History	1982	Sport & Leisure	Being out first ball
Culture & Belief	1801	Science & Tech	Flying saucers
Stage & Screen	They were brother and sister	True or False?	True

SET 93

Food & Drink
A gallon

Natural World
Copper and tin

History
The Bay of Pigs

Culture & Belief
St Andrews, Glasgow, Aberdeen, Edinburgh

Stage & Screen
David Jacobs

Written Word
Romeo

Music
De Libes

Famous People
Attlee, Wilson and Callaghan

Sport & Leisure
Essex

Science & Tech
Luddites

True or False?
True

SET 94

Food & Drink
Orchid

Natural World
Zambesi

History
Roosevelt, Stalin and Churchill

Culture & Belief
Dublin

Stage & Screen
George Lazenby

Written Word
Mycroft

Music
Cello

Famous People
Delano

Sport & Leisure
1

Science & Tech
The lines of the hand

True or False?
False (it was York)

SET 95

Written Word			The Great Gatsby
Food & Drink	X-rays or gamma rays	Music	Dizzy
Natural World	Dogfish	Famous People	Sullivan
History	Truman, Attlee and Stalin	Sport & Leisure	Lahore, Pakistan
Culture & Belief	Left a will	Science & Tech	One gallon
Stage & Screen	Berlin	True or False?	False (it's in Switzerland)

SET 96

Written Word			Jane
Food & Drink	Margarine	Music	Tears
Natural World	1500ml	Famous People	Crimean
History	Churchill	Sport & Leisure	22
Culture & Belief	Spain	Science & Tech	Dentist
Stage & Screen	Antiques dealer	True or False?	True

SET 97

Food & Drink	Sheep	Written Word	Leopold Bloom
Natural World	1953	Music	You find a girl to love
History	The Maginot line	Famous People	Ian Paisley
Culture & Belief	Gdansk	Sport & Leisure	Joe Davis and Fred Davis
Stage & Screen	Documentary	Science & Tech	Water
		True or False?	False (it was in 1947)

SET 98

Food & Drink	Mozzarella	Written Word	*Lord of the Rings*
Natural World	One's brother	Music	A reason to be cheerful
History	The majority	Famous People	Christopher Columbus
Culture & Belief	An officer of the order of the British Empire	Sport & Leisure	Ray Reardon, Steve Davis, Stephen Hendry
Stage & Screen	Venice (1932)	Science & Tech	Credit cards
		True or False?	True

SET 99

| Written Word | Typeface |

| Food & Drink | Parma |

| Music | Two |

| Natural World | Shipping forecast areas |

| Famous People | Runcie (all were Archbishops of Canterbury) |

| History | 1917 |

| Sport & Leisure | Snooker and billiards |

| Culture & Belief | Railway workers |

| Science & Tech | Self-Contained Underwater Breathing Apparatus |

| Stage & Screen | *Play Misty For Me* |

| True or False? | True |

SET 100

| Written Word | 1954/55/56 |

| Food & Drink | Potato |

| Music | Horsehair |

| Natural World | Colorado |

| Famous People | Oscar Wilde |

| History | His severed ear |

| Sport & Leisure | Tony Jacklin |

| Culture & Belief | Scotland |

| Science & Tech | By matching fingerprints |

| Stage & Screen | *High Noon* |

| True or False? | True |

SET 101

Food & Drink	Potatoes
Natural World	Six weeks
History	1938
Culture & Belief	St Francis of Assisi
Stage & Screen	*A Clockwork Orange*
Written Word	Garrison Keillor
Music	Green (manalishi/ tambourine/door)
Famous People	Natalia Markova
Sport & Leisure	Golf (it's a type of club)
Science & Tech	The sound barrier
True or False?	True (1 January)

SET 102

Food & Drink	Potatoes
Natural World	Salmon
History	Sydney
Culture & Belief	Turned it into wine
Stage & Screen	He was the first actor to be knighted
Written Word	Henry Root
Music	*(Let's Make Lots of Money)*
Famous People	Slavery
Sport & Leisure	Alan Shephard
Science & Tech	Velcro
True or False?	False (it was disobedience)

SET 103

Written Word	He bit off the dog's ear
Food & Drink	They're used as a laxative
Music	Steely Dan
Natural World	The Fair Isle
Famous People	Liverpool
History	Clergy, nobility, commoners
Sport & Leisure	Golf club
Culture & Belief	Scotland
Science & Tech	Ionic and Corinthian
Stage & Screen	Roger Moore
True or False?	False (it wasn't coined until 1966)

SET 104

Written Word	Iota
Food & Drink	Salt
Music	Jonathan King
Natural World	Sea horse
Famous People	Edward VIII
History	Hobby horse
Sport & Leisure	Pacho Gonzalez & Charlie Pasarell
Culture & Belief	Switzerland
Science & Tech	On a map of the world
Stage & Screen	Piccadilly Circus (1896)
True or False?	False

SET 105

Food & Drink	Oil is liquid, fat solid
Natural World	Hudson
History	Rudyard Kipling
Culture & Belief	Limerick
Stage & Screen	1965
Written Word	Schindler's Ark
Music	Mott the Hoople
Famous People	1909
Sport & Leisure	Ski-ing
Science & Tech	Nescafé
True or False?	True

SET 106

Food & Drink	Palm tree
Natural World	Bird droppings
History	17th
Culture & Belief	Heroes killed in battle
Stage & Screen	The Great Dictator
Written Word	A dance marathon
Music	Sal Solo
Famous People	The Royal Navy
Sport & Leisure	Men's tennis
Science & Tech	The first atomic bomb
True or False?	True

SET 107

Written Word	1949
Food & Drink	Perrier
Music	Air on a G String
Natural World	Dumfriesshire
Famous People	New York
History	Turkey
Sport & Leisure	Arsenal
Culture & Belief	Paul Channon
Science & Tech	Kleenex
Stage & Screen	1956
True or False?	True

SET 108

Written Word	Peter Benchley
Food & Drink	Perrier
Music	Buster Bloodvessel
Natural World	Stalagmites
Famous People	Fiji
History	Kowtow
Sport & Leisure	Bobby Jones
Culture & Belief	Ottoman
Science & Tech	Shredded Wheat
Stage & Screen	Robert Redford
True or False?	True

SET 109

Food & Drink	D	**Written Word**	Two
Natural World	Mars	**Music**	Matt Bianco
History	The Fabian Society	**Famous People**	Fingall
Culture & Belief	Canada	**Sport & Leisure**	One
Stage & Screen	Walter Matthau	**Science & Tech**	Hurricane
		True or False?	False (that was Joe Louis)

SET 110

Food & Drink	They grow above the ground	**Written Word**	Ursula K. le Guin
Natural World	A mule	**Music**	David Essex
History	Robespierre	**Famous People**	Al Capone's
Culture & Belief	The highwayman had a horse	**Sport & Leisure**	The Ascot Gold Cup
Stage & Screen	Lassie	**Science & Tech**	Libraries
		True or False?	False (every four)

SET 111

Food & Drink	Jennifer Paterson, Clarissa Dickson Wright
Natural World	St Helier
History	Car
Culture & Belief	Sitar
Stage & Screen	Tom Baker
Written Word	William (Willie)
Music	10538
Famous People	Jackie Kennedy
Sport & Leisure	John Spencer
Science & Tech	Architects
True or False?	False (it's a calf)

SET 112

Food & Drink	A can of coke
Natural World	By crushing
History	Man
Culture & Belief	New Zealand
Stage & Screen	Casablanca
Written Word	Humbert Humbert
Music	Jim Croce
Famous People	Gerald Ford
Sport & Leisure	Policeman
Science & Tech	Bakelite
True or False?	True

SET 113

Food & Drink	Bisto
Natural World	About two years
History	Ford
Culture & Belief	By flea bite
Stage & Screen	The city of Alexandria

Written Word	Tennessee Williams
Music	With a Girl Like You
Famous People	Duke of Wellington
Sport & Leisure	Ayr
Science & Tech	A car radio
True or False?	True

SET 114

Food & Drink	Wine
Natural World	A bat
History	Virginia
Culture & Belief	Hallowe'en
Stage & Screen	Bela Lugosi

Written Word	J. D. Salinger
Music	Toto
Famous People	Pope John Paul II
Sport & Leisure	Churchill Downs
Science & Tech	A car
True or False?	True

SET 115

| Written Word | The Catcher in the Rye |

| Food & Drink | Almond |

| Music | *It's All Over Now* |

| Natural World | Leveret |

| Famous People | Edwin (Buzz) Aldrin |

| History | 1989 |

| Sport & Leisure | The Prix de l'Arc de Triomphe |

| Culture & Belief | The Tudor rose |

| Science & Tech | *Hamlet*'s 'To be or not to be' |

| Stage & Screen | Tara King |

| True or False? | True |

SET 116

| Written Word | 14 |

| Food & Drink | Neapolitan |

| Music | *Carmen* |

| Natural World | The Balearics |

| Famous People | Ken Dodd |

| History | Light emitting diode |

| Sport & Leisure | 400m |

| Culture & Belief | Plato |

| Science & Tech | New York and Chicago |

| Stage & Screen | BAFTA |

| True or False? | False (it was Jochan Rindt) |

SET 117

Food & Drink	Colmans
Natural World	The Solent
History	300 metres
Culture & Belief	The town crier
Stage & Screen	British Academy of Film and Television Arts
Written Word	Tolkein
Music	*Move it*
Famous People	Highgate Cemetery, London
Sport & Leisure	McLaren-Mercedes
Science & Tech	Points of equal depth on sea charts
True or False?	True

SET 118

Food & Drink	Uruguay
Natural World	Ontario and Erie
History	240
Culture & Belief	Jubilee
Stage & Screen	The first Academy Awards (Oscars awards ceremony)
Written Word	The only fruit
Music	Muhammad Ali
Famous People	Lord Haw Haw
Sport & Leisure	Brands Hatch
Science & Tech	It was waterproof
True or False?	False (it's three years)

SET 119

Food & Drink	Textured vegetable protein	Written Word	Bertie Wooster
Natural World	Horseshoe Falls and Rainbow Falls	Music	Marie
History	British Telecom	Famous People	Raffles
Culture & Belief	£2 coin	Sport & Leisure	Cribbage
Stage & Screen	1700	Science & Tech	Blood bank
		True or False?	False (it was Franz Hals)

SET 120

Food & Drink	Sugar (caramelised)	Written Word	Willy Loman
Natural World	Orkney	Music	Neil Diamond
History	Spike Milligan	Famous People	Ho Chi Minh City
Culture & Belief	Harlequin	Sport & Leisure	*Bluebird*
Stage & Screen	13½ in (34 cm)	Science & Tech	Paper clips
		True or False?	True